Writing a Successful College Application Essay

The Key to College Admission

Third Edition • George Ehrenhaft

BARRON'S

For Dave, Ellie, and Sylvia

About the Author

George Ehrenhaft, a graduate of Columbia College and Ohio State, has taught students how to write successful college application essays for over three decades. He is the former head of the English Department at Mamaroneck High School and resides in Katonah, New York.

© Copyright 2000 by Barron's Educational Series, Inc.
Prior editions © Copyright 1993, 1987 by Barron's Educational Series, Inc.

All inquiries should be addressed to:

Barron's Educational Series, Inc.
250 Wireless Boulevard
Hauppauge, NY 11788
www.barronseduc.com

Library of Congress Catalog Card No. 00-023824

ISBN-13: 978-0-7641-1427-4
ISBN-10: 0-7641-1427-1

Library of Congress Cataloging-in-Publication Data

Ehrenhaft, George.
    Writing a successful college application essay : the key
to college admission / George Ehrenhaft. — 3rd ed.
        p.   cm.
    Includes index.
    ISBN 0-7641-1427-1 (alk. paper)
    1. College applications.   2. Exposition (Rhetoric)
3. Universities and colleges—Admission.   4. Academic writing.

LB2351.5 .E37   2000   00-023824
378.1'616—dc21   CIP

PRINTED IN CANADA

19   18   17   16   15   14   13   12   11   10

Table of Contents

ACKNOWLEDGMENTS

Scores of people have contributed to this book. Many are the high school students who populated my English classes for over three decades. They taught *me*, I believe, far more than I could ever have taught them about the craft of writing. From their stumbling but sincere writing efforts, I learned what it takes to make words clear, interesting, and correct. The lessons they taught me echo throughout these pages.

A college application essay offers a writing teacher the ultimate high. Perhaps for the first time, students write something that counts for more than just a grade in school. They see that skill in writing can make a difference in their lives, that words empower them to disturb the universe. For showing me the way, I'm indebted to Rose Scotch, Michael DiGennaro, and Susan Freeman. I also wish to thank Ileen Gottesfeld, Paul Martin, and Ettore Piraino for contributing their students' essays to the book.

I'm especially grateful to the dozens of students who consented to have their college essays reproduced—in whole or in part—throughout this volume. Most of the essays were written in Mamaroneck (NY) High School, but they also come from students attending Mahopac High School, Scarsdale High School, White Plains High School, John Jay High School in Cross River, NY, Horace Greeley High School in Chappaqua, NY, and the Berkshire School in Sheffield, Massachusetts.

The gracious volunteers in Mamaroneck's College Information Center gave expert help and provided a site for fruitful discussions with college admissions representatives from across the nation. A heartfelt thanks, too, to the dozens of deans and directors of admission who described how essays are used in making admissions decisions. I also appreciate the help of Mark Miele at Barron's.

I save my biggest hug for Al Greenberg, now at the American School in Milan, Italy. As Al talked to me about writing application essays, I realized that he probably should have written this book. In a sense, I became another of the countless students who have benefited from his insights and experience as a counselor.

Finally, to my wife Susan: Your support has been incalculable.

G.E.

Every college and university should ask
prospective students to submit an essay as
part of their application for admission not only
to underline the importance of writing but also as a
means of learning more about the needs as well as
the strengths of students.
—A recommendation from
*College: The Undergraduate
Experience in America,* a study of
education by the Carnegie Foundation for
the Advancement of Teaching

1 YOUR ESSAY MAKES A DIFFERENCE

Step into a fantasy world for a moment, and sit at the desk of a college admissions officer reviewing applications for next year's freshman class. Better still, play the role yourself. You've read about forty-five applications today, and you are down to your last three. Your colleagues have gone home. It's dark outside, and you are tired and hungry. The stack of rejected applications on your desk reaches almost to the level of your aching eyes. The "maybe" pile is half as tall. A wire basket marked "yes!" holds another stack barely three inches high.

At eight o'clock tomorrow the admissions committee will need your decisions. You carry an awesome burden on your shoulders—the destiny of real, live people. Each person comes from a good high school. Teachers and counselors have sent warm endorsements. None of the three has alumni connections—they'll sink or swim on their own. It's in your hands. What will you recommend? Admit? Wait-list? Reject?

> As an admissions officer, you carry a awesome burden on your shoulders—the destiny of real, live people.

Jeff G's papers show you that he has taken tough courses in high school and that he will graduate in the top ten percent of his class. You also note SAT I scores near 650 in both verbal and math, and participation in school life as a yearbook staffer, cross-country runner, and co-captain of the debate team.

Then you come to the essay question, which asks applicants to describe an important personal experience and explain its significance. Jeff's response is rather uninspired. It makes the point that involvement in various high school activities has taught him to be a serious-minded, hard-working, and responsible person. In college he expects to study hard and earn good grades.

Kathy E's application boasts several achievements in foreign languages. You observe that Kathy has won school certificates in Spanish and French and that she has also studied German. She plans to major in languages and hopes someday to work for the U.S. Department of State. Her overall average is 90 and her verbal SAT I score is 630. In school she joined the language clubs and helped to publish a foreign language newspaper.

1

Kathy's essay contains a list of European countries she visited during the last two summers and makes the point that, although travel is broadening and fun, there's no place like home.

Pat McM's application shows that he earned an 86 average in a generally rigorous academic program, including an AP history course. Scores on SAT I and SAT II tests are not distinguished, but still within the range for your college. Pat acted in high school drama productions, played the saxophone in the jazz band, and in 11th grade devoted considerable time to Students for a Clean Environment.

To answer the essay question, Pat wrote an imaginary conversation with God after the ozone layer had been completely destroyed and only a few human beings were left on the planet.

Three good students, three qualified candidates for admission to your college. A high average and varied activities strengthen Jeff's application. Kathy's special interest in language commends her strongly. Pat's commitment to outside activities compensates for his marginal numbers.

Which of them would you accept?

How Colleges Decide

"The first order of business for an admission committee is to examine how students used their academic opportunities," says Katie Fretwell, Director of Admission at Amherst. "We look at the rigor of the courses that each applicant selected through high school."

After checking your grades and courses, each college will take a slightly different path. Some turn to your recommendations from counselors and teachers, others to test results. Although nearly all colleges tell you to take SAT Is or ACTs, they don't all give the scores equal weight.

You won't spring to life for the admissions committee without a thoughtful, well-written essay.

How you spent time outside of class is crucial, too, because colleges seek people who have charged full speed ahead into life. They want students who will participate, who will help shape the life on campus or in the community. They judge you according to the depth of your involvement, not by the number of activities you've joined.

The reputation of your secondary school may also count. Colleges know which schools habitually send out high-achieving, energetic learners. In addition, colleges like a geographic blend, often favoring candidates from distant regions of the country.

An alumni connection sometimes helps, and a congenial interview also adds strength to your record, especially when you travel to the campus to meet an admissions official in person.

Each section of a college application adds another piece to your portrait. You won't spring to life for the admissions committee, though, without a thoughtful, well-written essay. The essay is a window into your mind and personality: Unlike an A– in chemistry or an 80 in English, it reveals your uniqueness—what you think about, what drives you, and to what you aspire. Of course, it demonstrates your writing ability, too. The gift of saying what you want to say the way you want to say it can compensate for a weakness in almost any other part of the application. Typically, an effective essay can go a long way to offset a mediocre SAT I score. In fact, if most applicants poured as much sweat into their essays as they do into SAT I preparation, admissions officials would be inundated with volumes of first-rate reading.

> Typically, an effective essay can go a long way to offset a mediocre SAT I score.

The Needs of the College

Although colleges use different screening procedures, their intent is always the same—to choose a mix of bright, confident, and positive people who will help to make the college a stimulating place for the next four years. "There's no such thing as an ideal candidate," says Jon Reider, Senior Associate Director of Admission at Stanford. "Rather, we try to pick an ideal class." Since the mix keeps changing, this year's "accept" may be next year's "reject."

> Colleges want a mix of bright, confident, and positive people.

Colleges' needs vary from time to time. Students blessed with particular talents as debaters, high-divers, cartoonists, dancers, or any skill presently in short supply on the campus may occasionally be admitted to meet a request from a coach or faculty advisor. If most of the drummers in a college's marching band are seniors, for example, you can bet that admissions people will be asked to keep a sharp lookout for academically qualified high school drummers.

Your chances of being accepted also depend on the number of people seeking admission that year. Demographic trends create ebbs and flows. A sharp decline in births during the '60s and '70s reduced the applicant pool seventeen years later. Fewer high school graduates to go around forced some colleges to swing their doors open a bit wider in the '80s and early '90s. Near the turn of the twenty-first century, however, the number of applicants swelled to record highs. A larger college-aged population, a roaring economy, the growing belief that a college education is necessary for success, even the use of the Internet, which made applying to college easier and faster than ever—all contributed to an annual flood of applications to colleges big and small.

Interest in particular colleges also rises and falls with the fortunes of its athletic teams. When a college wins a national basketball or football title, applications inevitably jump the following year. Richard Whiteside, the head of admissions at Tulane University, said that applications shot up almost 6 percent the year after Tulane's football team went undefeated. At Fairfield University, Mary Spiegel, the director of admissions, explains that the "recent success of the university's varsity teams" contributed to an 11 percent rise in applications.

As the tuition and other college costs rise to new heights each year, applications to selective, but cheaper, state colleges and universities rise too. The state colleges at Binghamton and Albany in the New York State system, for example, have grown far more competitive than many private colleges. The University of California campus at Berkeley has become more exclusive than Dartmouth, Penn, and other Ivy League colleges. Typically, during hard economic times expensive private colleges tend to relax admissions standards to make room for less-qualified students from affluent families.

Current events at home and abroad bear on college application statistics. When the Cold War ended, for instance, Congress reduced the enrollment at the Air Force, Army, and Naval academies by 10 percent. Consequently, applicants to the smaller service academies began to face the stiffest competition in years, on a par at least with applicants to such colleges as Cornell, Duke, and Notre Dame.

In New York City, long considered an unsafe and violent place, colleges strained to attract students from out of town. In the late 1990s, however, New York enjoyed a mini-Renaissance. As crime declined and the city cleaned up its act, Columbia, NYU, Barnard, and Fordham, as well as other New York schools, became so-called "hot" colleges. In six years, NYU's applicant pool grew 115 percent. In 1999 Columbia received 13,011 applications for 955 places in the freshman class. Accepting only 13.6 percent of its applicants, Columbia suddenly became more selective than Yale and Brown.

After Bill Clinton was elected to the presidency, applications to his alma mater, Georgetown University, jumped 11 percent. At the same time, applications to Wellesley College reached a record high, largely because of publicity about Hillary Rodham Clinton, a 1969 graduate who often speaks affectionately about her student days at Wellesley.

Even widely read college reference books, such as *Peterson's 4 Year Colleges 2000* and *The Fiske Guide to Colleges,* can influence the number of applications. Washington University, for instance, got a lift when Barron's *Profiles of American Colleges* reclassified the college from "highly competitive" to "most competitive," the equivalent of adding a fourth star to a three-star rating.

The Admissions Committee at Work

Accept? Wait-list? Reject? Thousands of decisions every year—each made thoughtfully and humanely, with complete awareness that a concerned applicant is waiting for a verdict.

What would you tell Jeff, Kathy, and Pat? The majority of colleges in the United States would probably admit all three without hesitation, glad to have attracted applicants of such high caliber. But more selective schools would screen them with agonizing care before deciding. An admissions committee may assign numerical ratings to each candidate's academic and personal qualities. Two committee members may read each folder and make a recommendation. Difficult folders may be passed around the committee for a group decision. At the University of Chicago, up to seven people read the entire application.

Perhaps only 175 of nearly 2,000 four-year colleges in the United States choose their students with such agonizing care. In a recent year, highly competitive Middlebury College, for instance, accepted just 1,412 of its 4,436 applicants. Yale accepted fewer than 2,200 of the 12,046 who applied, and Stanford only 2,508 of 18,888— fewer than one in seven. Although the numbers differ and vary slightly from year to year, the admissions picture is similar at selective schools all across the country.

Only 175 of nearly 2,000 colleges in the U.S. receive three or more applications for each place in the freshman class.

Even at colleges where the competition isn't quite as intense, admissions people take pains to assemble a varied and qualified student body. A few colleges, struggling to stay in business, admit virtually anyone who applies, and others, bound by law, employ open admissions. Such schools are the exception. As a rule, selectivity is practiced everywhere, and the screening of applicants is never done haphazardly.

Colleges immediately eliminate anyone who clearly can't do the work. "In general," says Muhlenberg's dean of admission, Christopher Hooker-Haring, "students do a pretty good job of matching themselves up with colleges." As a result, 85 to 90 percent are academically qualified and survive the first cut. Next, a college may pick out a small group of superstars, from presidential scholars to world-class swimmers. The balance of candidates are left in what Harry Bauld, a former admissions representative at Brown and Columbia, terms "the gray area." These applicants, Bauld says, are "in the ball park" but still far from being accepted. Faced with large numbers of good scholastic records—like those submitted by Jeff, Kathy, and Pat—admissions officials make decisions using what Karl M. Furstenberg, dean of admissions at Dartmouth calls "the intangibles," qualities that don't show up on a transcript and can't be listed in a résumé. "This makes our job harder," claims Furstenberg. "It forces us to look at critical thinking." And nowhere is an applicant's level of thinking more evident than in the essay.

The Application Essay

"The essay can make the difference between a *wait-list* and an *admit* or a *wait-list* and a *deny*," says Jennifer Stein, who reads candidates' essays in the Connecticut College admissions office. "It can tip the balance, giving students an extra edge, or it can work against them." Jonathan Reider, Senior Associate Director of Admission at Stanford, concurs. The essay can play "a crucial role in deciding who among well-qualified applicants are the most compelling candidates for admission." Admissions dean Christopher Hooker-Haring of Muhlenberg, adds, "A terrible essay can sometimes prevent an otherwise

> "The essay can tip the balance," says Connecticut College.

qualified applicant from being admitted. And, for those applicants right on the margin, a strong essay can be the difference between admission and a spot on the waiting list."

At Williams three admissions people read and discuss every essay. A group of three to seven readers at the University of Chicago usually comment on each essay's style, complexity, and content. At Stanford, four or five admissions people may review an application and read the essay. "It's *that* important," says Reider.

Around the conference table in admissions offices, the essay often serves as the wild card, the piece of an application that may give an edge to a student like Pat McM. Writing a conversation with God shows that Pat has the courage to take intellectual and creative risks. Pat's approach is unique, and it confirms his interest in environmental issues. That he wrote a dialogue may suggest that his drama experience has left an enduring mark on the way he thinks. In short, he put himself into his writing.

On the other hand, Jeff G and Kathy E didn't. Both wrote proper, but boring, essays, which couldn't be distinguished from hundreds of others. Jeff's "what-I-did-in-high-school-and-what-I-learned-from-it" approach is common and uninspired. So is Kathy's conclusion. Kathy roamed Europe, but brought back a cliché. By submitting dull essays, both Jeff and Kathy have tarnished otherwise sterling records and have jeopardized their chances of getting into a selective college.

Marlyn McGrath Lewis, the Harvard admissions director, believes that the essay provides "an opportunity for the students to project a clearer sense of what makes them tick—their interests, background, even their personality." Students can reveal their uniqueness in an essay, reflect on their lives, and display their creativity. It's a place on the college application form where students have freedom to be creative and even have some fun.

Fun is serious business in college admissions. No, it's not a constant party inside the admissions offices at Johns Hopkins, Northwestern, and Duke. But those are a few of the schools that frequently revise their application forms to inspire more interesting essays. Among other colleges, the University of Chicago and Stanford try to change their questions every year. Essay readers want to enjoy their work, and they do a better job if each batch of essays responds to a fresh question. Hoping to make their work more enjoyable, MIT officials tell applicants to recognize that those who read their essays "will not mind being entertained." Also, each class takes on a distinct identity. Prospective

> Fun is serious business in college admissions.

members of American University's class of 2004 were asked to imagine themselves as editors of major newsmagazines and to write the cover story for the issue dated January 1, 2010. Applicants to Bennington are invited to invent their own question and answer it. Admissions people at the University of Pennsylvania realized that by asking the same old questions they got the same old answers. Therefore, they replaced a conventional "definition of success" question with a more sprightly one: You've just written a 300-page autobiography; please submit page 217 with this application.

At colleges with less vigorous admissions standards, officials also read application essays attentively. Like their associates at the hottest colleges, they seek the best, most promising, and vibrant students they can find. Although the essays may not always count as heavily in admissions decisions, officials sometimes use writing samples to place students in the proper academic program. The University of Michigan tells applicants that if they are accepted and enroll, their academic advisors will read their essays. "The essay will be used to help your advisor to become acquainted with you and to assist you in your educational planning." Furthermore, the essays help colleges see each applicant more clearly and personally. For example, an essay may explain why a bright student earned mediocre grades in high school, or it may reveal how a family or financial problem prevented an applicant from participating in school or community activities. In addition, a college official can often tell from an essay whether the applicant may be eligible for a restricted scholarship or other type of special aid. Eventually, essays wind up in the college files. Sometimes teachers, administrators, and counselors turn to application essays for helpful background information about their students.

Still, colleges of all stripes are most impressed by a student's academic performance. A perfect essay—even if such a thing existed—doesn't make up for less-than-brilliant grades or a transcript full of snap courses. Yet, nothing on the application wields as much power as a forceful essay. Poignant personal stories have pushed admissions committees to the verge of tears. But you can bet that no admissions officer has ever wept over an applicant's list of part-time jobs.

Write Your Way into College

A recent study by the National Association of College Admissions Counselors found that most of America's selective colleges choose

> By giving the essay all you've got, you could actually write your way into college.

students by their grades in college prep courses, by admissions test scores, recommendations, and *their ability to write the application essay.* In fact, over half of the colleges give the essay "considerable" to "moderate" weight in admission decisions. Jennifer Blair, an associate director of admissions at Marlboro College, ranks the essay as the second most important criterion after academic record. That is, after grades and difficulty of course load. Nevertheless, college officials say that many applicants don't seem to work very hard on their essays. Nearly half the essays submitted to Marietta College are "poorly done," according to the director of admissions, Marke Vickers. Cornell admissions officers believe that a majority of applicants think that good grades, test scores, and recommendations will unlock the college gates for them. They send in muddled essays, not realizing that by giving the essay all they've got, they might actually write their way into college. "That's too bad," says Dean Hooker-Haring of Muhlenberg. "It means that most students are missing a terrific opportunity to reach out from the pages of their applications, grab an admissions officer by the lapels, and say, "Here I am! This is why I belong at your college!"

The essay has not always borne such weight. In the past, the most selective colleges ranked the essay no higher than seventh or eighth among a dozen admissions criteria. The reason, theorized Georgetown's dean of admissions, was that many students couldn't write a decent paragraph. Half of the strongest candidates, the dean added, would be turned away if they had been judged on their writing alone. Today, the teaching of writing is a priority in schools everywhere, and writing instruction has improved. High school juniors and seniors have been writing stories and essays ever since kindergarten, and according to evaluations done periodically by the National Assessment of Educational Progress, the writing skills of seventeen-year-olds around the country, contrary to a popular myth, have not declined. Still, as Carol A. Rowlands, Director of Admissions at Lafayette, points out, "Each year we see a few essays that have clearly been thrown together at the last minute, reflecting negatively on the candidate."

Demands for writing essays vary from college to college. Most colleges, among them Boston University, Northwestern, and Tulane, require one essay. For others, such as Duke and the University of Vermont, applicants must write two or three short pieces in addition to one main essay. Bard, Colby, and Harvard ask for two essays, each between 250 and 500 words. Both MIT and Sarah

Lawrence want three pieces of writing. Princeton applicants must write four half-page essays. Rensselaer Polytechnic Institute requires one essay, but the topics vary according to the students' anticipated major. Future dentists write on different subjects than future lawyers and architects. Some colleges, such as Hampshire and Reed, ask applicants to submit not only an essay but a paper written for a high school course, complete with teacher comments and grade.

By asking prospective students to submit a writing sample as part of their application, colleges underscore the notion that good writing skills are a mark of an educated person. Colleges also use writing samples to assess strengths and weaknesses of their students. If half of an incoming class submits essays lacking a main idea or short on supporting detail, for example, the college will know exactly what it ought to be teaching in its freshman writing courses.

> Good writing skills are the mark of an educated person.

Although the nation's choices colleges ask prospective students for a writing sample, many of the less competitive colleges don't—sometimes because they don't have the staff to read even one-page essays. State universities such as those in Minnesota, Rhode Island, and Delaware, for instance, don't require essays. The University of Virginia, though, with 16,000 applicants a year, does. So do the University of Michigan and the University of Connecticut. At the University of California in Berkeley, a large team of people reads the annual flood of 30,000 applications. At some private colleges, faculty members join admissions personnel in marathon reading sessions.

At every college that requires an essay, you can depend on one thing: Essays are read thoughtfully. At Bennington, Bryn Mawr, and Smith, where the essay carries as much weight as any other part of the application, committees discuss applicants' writing at length. When admissions people convene for all-day sessions at Wesleyan, they guard against careless reading by taking frequent breaks. An application that surfaces late in the afternoon is read as respectfully as one at nine o'clock in the morning.

Although finding your way into the right college may seem like traversing a labyrinth, hundreds of thousands of students make the trip every year. At times the admissions system may appear fickle and unpredictable, almost beyond understanding. Yet, it works. As a college-bound student, you took your first steps toward your destination years ago when you learned to read and write and to compute numbers. You've studied, worked, and contributed in

---

In your essay, show the admissions staff you're too good to turn down.

---

some way to your school and community. You've taken College Board tests or ACTs and established your school record. You narrowed your college preferences, and perhaps had an interview or two.

By the time you fill in your name on your first application, the facts about you—for better or worse—are in. You can't change them. However, the opportunities in your essay are wide open. In your answers to the essay questions you have the chance to sparkle, to show the admissions staff that you're too good to turn down. Let the essay work for you. The remainder of this book will help you do it.

2 ESSAYS THAT WORK

In a survey about "life's ten most anxious moments," a majority of high school seniors agreed that getting up to talk in front of a group provoked the most anxiety. Second was applying to college, especially writing the essay.

It's easy to see why. The two tasks—addressing a group and composing an essay for a college application—have a lot in common. In both cases success depends on how well you present yourself, what you have to say, and how effectively you convey your message. Few people don't feel at least a little stage fright before facing an audience, and it's equally natural to feel edgy about filling up an empty sheet of paper with an essay that could clear or block your entry to your college of choice.

In a note to high school seniors on the verge of writing their personal essays, the Cornell application says, "We realize that you may approach the personal application . . . with some apprehension. That's understandable." Essay instructions on the William and Mary application say, in part, "Take your time, and try to have some fun with these essays." Princeton advises students filling out one part of its application, *"Please don't lose any sleep over the answers to this question."* It's nice of the colleges to be so understanding, but it's hard to be encouraged when all at the same time you're applying to several colleges (each demanding a different essay), you're trying to keep your grades up, and you're finding every week just too darn short!

Annette R, a high school senior interested in Saint Lawrence University, dealt with the pressure by trying to guess what the admissions office would expect her to write in response to the charge, "Describe a significant experience or achievement that has special meaning for you." She searched the college's web page for clues to what the college might like and found a special program called "Service Learning" that fosters good citizenship "through the development of a sense of responsibility for the welfare of others." "OK," Annette concluded, "if they like social do-gooders, I'll give them a social do-gooder." So she set out to prove that she and Saint Lawrence were meant for each other. She began her essay:

> Success depends on how well you present yourself, what you have to say and how effectively you convey your message.

> Your web site said that Service Learning program develops a sense of responsibility for the welfare of others. I would like

to attend Saint Lawrence because that description fits me perfectly. I am the type of person who likes people. I have many friends that I love dearly. I cannot walk the hallways of the high school without saying hello to someone. I am very happy that I have so many friends, and feel that I have so many because of my job. My job helps me to relate to people.

The balance of the essay described her job as a receptionist in a dentist's office, where she often comforted people in pain.

Annette had the academic credentials for Saint Lawrence, but was rejected. She had made the fatal mistake of trying to guess what she thought the college wanted, an approach always filled with peril. Admissions people don't want anything in particular except to have applicants write something that accurately portrays themselves. There are no hidden answers to the questions. Applicants "shouldn't try to figure out what a school is looking for," says Harvard/Radcliffe's admissions director Marlyn McGrath Lewis. "They should just try to convey a real and memorable sense of themselves." Lewis's words are echoed in the essay instructions from Bennington, which say, "The best advice we can offer is that you *not* try to give us what you think we want to hear. We don't know what we want to hear; we do know that we want to hear *you*." Thus, when a college asks, "Who belongs on a modern-day Mount Rushmore?"—as William and Mary once did—there really is no correct answer.

> Annette made the mistake of trying to guess what the college wanted.

Write Honestly About Yourself

In an essay about a "rewarding experience," Susan E gave Yale an honest self-portrait. She wrote about her audition for a summer school in the arts. "The tryouts," Susan said, "were not unlike writing a college essay":

Acting is, after all, the art of revealing character, and that is what I am trying to do now: present a clear picture of Susan E's character . . . so, if you don't mind, I'm going to think of this whole affair as an audition.

Actually, my experience with acting auditions is very limited. The most memorable and important audition I have ever had was for a summer theater program that I attended after my junior year. There were two auditions, a semifinal and a final round, and each time I performed two dramatic monologues. I created other people's characters and spoke other people's words. Thinking back on the experience, I believe my own character and my own words would have been infinitely more interesting. . . .

Susan then quoted the monologue she recited and describes what she felt after the audition:

There's the tremendous feeling of accomplishment. I suppose that's a big part of it—the accomplishment. I don't imagine performing would stimulate me so much if I had no success at it. In fact, if I were lousy at it, I probably would stay clear of it as much as possible—like gym. . . . Yeah, failure generally stinks. It's very scary to fail. In fact, right about now I'm going to start the seemingly unending process of contemplating this audition. "Did it go well? Did I say too much? Was I too honest? Did I sound silly? Will they laugh about this for weeks to come?"—Paranoia strikes deep, but fear of failure strikes deeper. Then I'll go the other way: "Of course they liked you. Honesty is refreshing. It took guts to be silly and they'll respect you for it." Well, I guess I'll know soon enough.

There's more, but by now you must have noticed that there's an honest-to-goodness person writing the words here. Susan's essay could be an entry in her diary—it's that personal. It's the kind of writing that helps admissions personnel to set one applicant apart from the others. In fact, that's the whole point, says Carol A. Rowlands, director of admissions at Lafayette. "An essay should distinguish one applicant from another."

Write About Something Important to You

Colleges ask for an essay largely because they want to get to know you. When the admissions staff has finished your essay, they should have a vivid sense of your personality. If you give them only what you think they want, you're being dishonest, posing as someone you are not. An imposter may try to pass himself off in his essay as a seriously committed poet, for example. But if the rest of his application makes no reference to writing poetry, or working on publications, or taking poetry courses, readers may think twice about accepting his word. Consistency helps. Admissions officials often cite cases of students who write impassioned essays about racism, sweatshop labor, the plight of the homeless, gun laws, and other timely issues. Yet nothing in the students' records shows a particular interest in human rights, in politics, or in any current issues for that matter. Topics seem to have been pulled from the op-ed pages of newspapers.

Application essays are not meant to demonstrate your knowledge of current events. They have an altogether different purpose. As Perry Robinson of Denison University's admissions office says, "We want to know how well students write and whether they can address a given topic. We also hope to find out who they are, what's important to them, and why."

John E. Stafford, a counselor at Byram Hills High School (NY), tells his students, "Pick a topic you care about, an issue of significance and familiarity to you." Why? Because nothing will flop faster than an impersonal essay full of sweeping generalizations about a big issue that has puzzled experts and politicians for years.

> Before you write about the homeless, serve dinner in a downtown shelter.

If you're going to write about the homeless, make sure you can demonstrate real knowledge and personal interest. Have you, for example, served dinner in a downtown shelter, collected clothing for homeless families, or at least spoken out about the subject in your history class? Monica Barbano, a former admissions official at Muhlenberg, advises, "Write about something you feel strongly about, something you're passionate about—and not only will you be excited about it, so will we."

Andy C, applying to Boston University, tripped on a one-and-a-half page essay about the state of planet Earth that began this way:

> In this day and age environmental problems are very important worldwide topics of discussion. These controversial issues have a great effect on all of society. . . . I am very concerned about what is happening to our habitat.

Andy was probably sincere, perhaps even gravely worried about global pollution, but there is nothing personal or persuasive about his concern.

Harry Bauld, a former admissions dean at Brown and Columbia, says that those vague statements that go on and on about pollution, AIDS, or world hunger are called "Miss America" essays. Like beauty queens, they recite platitudes and offer simple-minded solutions to the stickiest problems. "I think the conflict between pro-life and pro-choice could be solved if both sides just sat down and had a good heart-to-heart talk," wrote one "contestant" in an application sent to Boston University.

Northwestern recently asked applicants to name a creative work that would reveal something about them. Assistant Director of Admission Charles Cogan reports that "literally hundreds of students picked *Great Expectations,* while another substantial group picked *The Little Engine That Could.* The first choice told us very little about the applicants, except that they were ambitious and wanted to get into a top school (also that they were reading Dickens). The second, while still far too common, had an undertone of 'I'll do whatever it takes to succeed at Northwestern.' What neither response did was to differentiate one student from another."

In contrast, Inga K, applying to Johns Hopkins, laid claim to a serious interest in Finnish politics at the outset of an essay on the Finnish economy:

> Through my mother I am a Finnish citizen. She came from Finland and thought it would be a good idea for her children to hold dual citizenship. . . .
>
> Even though I am very Americanized, I still have strong ties to Finland. At home I often speak Finnish, I eat Finnish food, read Finnish magazines, and even listen to the news from Helsinki on a shortwave radio. Although I have a lot of American friends, I'm closer to the Finnish friends I have at my church. Each summer I go to Finland for about a month to visit my relatives. When I am older, I may go to there to live. I don't know yet.
>
> Lately, I have been watching closely the Finnish economy and the consequences of . . .

"The best essays," says Susan Wertheimer of the University of Vermont admissions office, "come directly from the heart. Too often, students think we want to read only about 'big' themes or major life events. That's not so. The most memorable essay I read last year was composed by a young woman who described her feelings when her best friend moved away. The topic was simple— a common experience in today's mobile culture. I understood how she felt, why the friendship had meant so much to her, how she'd coped with the loss and moved on in her life."

Write a Unique Essay—the One That Only You Can Write

Even essays on topics of vital personal interest don't guarantee success, of course. Sometimes you can hardly tell one from the other. They sound almost mass-produced. "We don't expect Pulitzer Prize essays," says Karen Ley, a former admissions associate at Lafayette, "just good honest efforts that tell us something about the individual writer."

When he began his essay for the Air Force Academy, Tom M didn't realize the pitfalls of assembly-line writing:

> I would like to attend the Air Force Academy because I want a good college education. I also want to learn to fly, become a military officer and serve my country.

"So do 8,000 other applicants," Tom's high school English teacher told him. "What's going to set you apart from every other candidate?" It was fortunate that Tom ran his essay through several drafts. His first effort would certainly have earned him a letter of rejection because it lacked a hook to catch the eye of an admissions official. Much later, after numerous drafts, Tom had a hook:

> "Five. Four. Three. Two. One. Blast off!"
> My friend Eric pushed the button and a red rocket, about as long as my forearm and less than half as wide, whooshed into the sky. It almost disappeared from view before we saw the opening of a small white parachute that would bring it safely back to earth. "Wow-eee," Eric and I shouted as we sprinted toward the landing site as fast as our eleven-year-old legs would move. Another successful launch by the founders and only members of the Linden Street Junior Birdman Club!

Tom then recalls that his love affair with flying sprouted during his days as a rocket maniac in sixth grade. Although Tom finally decided not to apply to the Air Force Academy, the magnetism of his new opening paragraph may well have stopped his folder from slipping unnoticed into the rejection pile.

Jim R, an applicant to Duke, responding to the question, "What is it you do that best reflects your personality?" devised a uniquely personal approach. He wrote a list of forty sentences, each beginning with *I*:

> I love music of every kind.
> I have never been rock-climbing, but I intend to go soon.
> I share a room with my kid brother who is a dirt-bike maniac and who often drives me up the wall.
> I hate to sit in front of people who talk in the movies.
> I grow weepy over stories of faithful dogs like Lassie and Buck.
> I could survive very well on a diet of spaghetti and Dr. Pepper.

Thirty-four sentences later, no reader could fail to recognize Jim, the person behind the essay.

When a college asks you to describe your interests, be cautious. Don't let your passion for karate, military history, or sailing distract you from the purpose of the essay—to tell the college about yourself. Stay clear of the temptation to write a *World Book* article on black belts, famous battles, or boats. Matt S couldn't resist writing about the subject he loved the most. He began (and continued) in this fashion:

> One of my main interests is cartography. Some day I hope to work for the U.S. Coast and Geodetic Survey, the federal agency responsible for making and maintaining maps for the government and the public. Mapmaking is fascinating, especially because maps keep changing. Most people think that the land never changes, but with road construction, dams, floods, earthquakes, storms and fires, many maps made forty or fifty years ago are now obsolete. One of the most dramatic cartographic changes in the United States has been on Cape Cod, Massachusetts. Every decade the ocean coastline recedes thirty feet and the bay shoreline grows a similar amount. The place where the pilgrims landed in 1620 is now a quarter of a mile offshore.

Few high school students study maps as avidly as Matt. In spite of his unusual passion, however, his essay sounds much like a geography textbook. It fails to convey the qualities that colleges look for in application essays: ability to think on an abstract level, resilience, empathy, and a whole host of other *personal* characteristics.

Focus on a Single Area

Matt hid his personality in facts and statistics. Nevertheless, he had the good sense to focus his essay on a single topic. Not everyone does. Here, for example, is the opening of Nancy B's essay for Ohio Wesleyan:

> My four years in high school have been very rewarding and productive. As well as receiving excellent grades, I have become involved in many of the extracurricular activities offered at the school. Although at times I have been dissatisfied with some of my classes, I am generally enthusiastic about activities, and this enthusiasm has added a lot of life to the school atmosphere.
>
> In addition to academic achievements, I have developed a strong sense of leadership. This is evident in the positions I have held during the past four years as elected representative to the school government, captain of the lacrosse team, co-chair of the assemblies committee and editor-in-chief of the yearbook. . . .

Don't repeat in your essay what you've written someplace else on your application.

Because Nancy had already listed her activities on the application, she squandered a chance to give Ohio Wesleyan more information about herself. She buried a lively personality in an essay that reads like a list of activities. Shirley Levin, an educational consultant from Rockville, Maryland, says, "It's far better to convey a feeling of pride, achievement, or accomplishment in a very small area."

Elissa G did just that in her Bryn Mawr application. Long a frustrated math student, she focused sharply on her ultimate victory over arithmetic, as this excerpt shows:

> . . . I never did get the hang of adding anything with more than one digit. I still have to think twice when multiplying six and eight. Moreover, I am completely reliant on my pencil and

paper. The most annoying facet of this whole disability is that I understand and like math. Algebraic theory fascinated me, geometric proofs thrilled me and logarithms were amazing. Yet, I kept messing up tests and problems because I multiplied wrong, or added wrong or subtracted wrong . . . thank heaven for partial credit! Finally, in my sophomore year, I was rewarded for my rudimentary deficiencies. After maintaining a B average in my Trig class for a whole year, I whizzed the Regents, got a 100 and received an A in the course.

Focusing on a single area may be tough when you've done a lot with your life. By targeting one activity, though, you can show how hard you've thrown yourself into it. You can also include specific details about yourself, details that make you sound more like a real person. Consider, for example, this excerpt from Susan F's essay for Brown University:

My most rewarding acting experience was at the Andover Summer Session. I played the ruinous young girl, Mary Tilford, in Lillian Hellman's *The Children's Hour*. The role was very different from those I was accustomed to, like the good-natured nurse, Nellie Forbush, in *South Pacific*. Mary is a sadistic, tantrum-throwing, spoiled child who can also present a most ingenuous exterior. To show her complex personality—the manipulative female, the affectionate grandchild, the nasty friend—was difficult for me. I have a tendency to repress all anger, and when Mary was alone with her peers she was vicious. In one scene I had to slap a girl who is a good friend. To make the slap believable I had to really hit her. This was almost harder than the hysterics or the cloying sweetness, but with practice was finally perfected. To my pleasure, some of the audience did take my portrayal seriously. I had several students stop me in the cafeteria and with horrified expressions exclaim, "You're so mean!" Fiction had been transformed into reality—perhaps the best review.

The Boasting Problem

Susan wanted Brown to know of her triumph on the stage. She was rightfully proud of her accomplishment, yet didn't sound

Be proud of your achieve-
ments, but don't brag.

boastful. Since most of us have been taught not to boast, we don't usually puff ourselves up too much. We don't want to appear conceited. Still, Shirley Levin tells college applicants, "Look, if you don't blow your horn, nobody else will." The problem, though, is that self-impressed people rarely impress others. So, if you're good at something, tell the college, of course, but don't shout. A champion with a touch of reserve or a sense of humor is always more endearing than a braggart.

Mike M is a gifted political cartoonist, justifiably proud of his accomplishments. He injects droll humor into all his drawings. Yet in this passage from his New York University essay, which focuses on his gift, he sounds smug, maybe even arrogant:

> I would like to direct the attention of the admissions committee to my extensive involvement in political cartooning for the past four years. The responsibility of producing no less than one satirical drawing per week has necessitated my regular reading of *The New York Times* and other news publications, such as *Time* and *USA Today*. As a consequence, I have become well-informed on issues of national affairs and American foreign policy. In the future, I anticipate using my knowledge and artistic talent to raise the social consciousness of the ordinary citizen by pointing out the issues that I feel are of great importance.

Mike was accepted, but surely not for being the sort of person his essay portrays.

Similarly, a high school senior named Eliot M, evidently dazzled by his own musical achievement, didn't realize how immodest he sounded when he told Tufts:

> My extraordinary talent and accomplishments in the field of music are sufficiently noteworthy to warrant my inclusion in the highly selective all-county orchestra.

Although Eliot may deserve respect for his musicianship, he could probably use a lesson in modesty.

Actually, modesty is rather easy to learn. Just say that you consider yourself lucky to have great talent, or after telling how you've struggled to attain success, add that you're still trying to do better. For instance, Suzanne W, another exceptional musician, wrote on her Yale application:

> As a violinist, I have discovered wonderful feelings of accomplishment, surpassed only by the knowledge that it is only the beginning of a lifetime's experience.

Roger D is also blessed with excellence. He loves art and knows a lot about it. In his Columbia essay, he showed how well informed he is by relating an incident in the art museum:

> As I was standing in front of *St. Francis in Ecstasy*, two college students came over and started discussing the painting because they had to answer questions about its symbolism, composition and use of color for their art history class. Realizing that they weren't getting very far on their own, I decided to help. I pointed out religious symbolism and mentioned Giovanni Bellini's influence on Venetian painting—his use of sensuous colors and perspective. They seemed impressed by what I said, and I don't know which I enjoyed more—talking about the painting or looking at it.

The simple phrase, "I don't know," rescues Roger from sounding vain. More than that, though, he got a kick out of using his knowledge to do a good turn for someone else.

Of course, excessive pride may not be your problem. Like most people, perhaps, you don't have an exceptional talent. In fact, you may be searching for something in your life that's worth writing about. Don't worry. Everyday life has been the source of many outstanding essays. In your school locker, in your work as a checker at ShopRite, in your close ties to a grandparent, you may find kindling for a good, sharply focused essay. For Tufts, Dave K wrote about delivering newspapers to lonely senior citizens. Every day he became an old woman's link to the world. Kenny D, applying to Michigan, described his fight against boredom as a stock clerk at a supermarket. As he unpacked boxes he became a student of shopping carts, discovering that consumers express themselves by their choice of groceries.

Dangerous Areas:
Proceed with Caution

The "Jock" Essay

Although no essay topic is off limits, some contain pitfalls that you should avoid. Admissions personnel, for instance, are rarely impressed by the so-called jock essay, the one that predictably tells the reader what you learned from being first-string left tackle or playing goalie on the field hockey team. Every reasonably successful athlete has learned self-discipline, courage, and sportsmanship on the field. If a sport has truly been a crucial part of your life, your essay will have to show how. However, you'll have to do more than write the story of how winning the race made you feel, or how losing it helped to build your character.

In her application essay for the University of North Carolina, Alison L, a sprinter on the track team who suffers from exercise-induced asthma, wrote that "the word 'fun' had no place in the lexicon of track terms, while the phrase 'welcome to Hell' found itself right at home." Her essay details the agony of daily practice but then bursts with gratitude for all the benefits she derived from pushing herself to the limit:

> It is said that the strength of effort is the measure of the result, and by golly, I must have made one heck of an effort because the long-term results are wonderful and abundant. The most significant effect is the impact track has made on my health. While running, I could not conceive how the strain I was placing on my already burdened lungs could possibly improve my condition, but I soon realized that intense training expanded my lung capacity, increased my endurance, improved my muscular strength, and on top of it all, caused me to lose thirteen excess pounds.

Alison adds that track improved her performance in school, too. Before track, she procrastinated and always rushed to complete homework at the last minute. "While on the team," she wrote, "I was forced to finish assignments many days prior to the due date, in anticipation of lengthy track meets."

Brian C, a fencer, wrote a more dramatic jock essay for the University of Pennsylvania. As these excerpts show, Brian invites you into his mind during a match:

"Fencers, ready?"

"Ready, sir."

"Fence!"

. . . . I must win this bout. I have to be careful; I must find and exploit his weakness without allowing him to ensnare me with his strength. Every fencing bout starts like an argument: In the beginning, one must be patient and find out where one's opponent stands on the issue, before going in for the kill. When I was a child I would always lose arguments. Afterward I would go home and think of things I could have said to win. When I entered high school, I joined Model Congress, an organization patterned on the U.S. Congress. After three years, it has improved my verbal fencing immeasurably and I find that now I rarely lose an argument.

. . . He advances; I retreat, extend, lunge and miss. He moves in for the riposte. Panicking, I make a wild parry; he coolly disengages and I feel his point on my chest.

"Halt!" yells the director. "Touch left. Score is 3–1. Fencers ready?"

I am upset. He's scored three times as many touches on me as I have on him. If the bout continues like this, I will lose! This sport is silly; poking people with metal blades! I could be reading a book now. Reading is a wonderful pastime because every time I read I learn something new. When I read, I empathize with the characters. I feel new feelings and think new thoughts. Every book I read makes me more complete.

As he thrusts and parries, Brian also thinks about skiing, sailing, doing his physics homework, and traveling. In fewer than 500 words, Brian's personality and interests unfold. He reveals his intellect and sense of humor, his versatility, and writing skill. Because he wrote a multidimensional self-portrait, Brian has strengthened his application. After reading the essay, an admissions committee would have little difficulty deciding whether Brian belonged in their college.

Last Summer I Went to . . .

At almost any college, Brian's essay would outclass most others, especially those written on such common topics as athletics, working as a camp counselor, a wilderness adventure, and travel. Traveling, in fact, is probably the most popular subject chosen for

Travel is probably the most popular subject for college application essays.

college essays. Applicants seem extraordinarily fond of turning their travels into "significant experience" stories. Travel has virtues galore, but writing about it can be perilous. Colleges take a dim view of essays that are little more than personal narratives of "My Trip to Niagara Falls" or "What I Learned About Myself While Biking the Berkshires." The admissions offices at the University of Virginia and other colleges report that one out of every five essays seems to be about travel. Karen Ley, formerly on the admissions staff at Lafayette, remembers reading thirty accounts of summer trips in a single day. "I never knew that travel could be so tedious," she says.

Once in a while, though, someone writes a gem of a travel essay, like this one that David M sent to Berkeley:

> My German teacher, Mr. Turner, has decorated his classroom with Lufthansa posters showing scenes of the Black Forest, fairy-tale castles on the Rhine and the mountains of Bavaria. There's also a beautiful sunset in Cologne, with the cathedral silhouetted against the orange sky. They are all hung there to show what we would see if we traveled to Germany, which I did last summer.
>
> In preparing for my trip I packed my 35 mm camera and a dozen rolls of color film. I wanted to be ready to take photos of all the picturesque sights we would encounter during our three-week trip. Strangely, I came back to the United States with ten rolls of film still in their boxes.

In the rest of his essay, David tells of how his attitude toward photography changed after meeting an elderly Dutchman, Mr. Gillem, in the memorial museum at Dachau, the site of a World War II concentration camp. Gillem, an art historian, talked with David at length about the uses of photography and convinced him that taking snapshots of pretty scenes merely wasted film. Pointing to photos depicting the horrors of the Holocaust, he told David to use his talent to awaken people to the wrongs of the world and to leave the scenery to postcard photographers. David closed with this paragraph:

> I took just forty pictures on my trip, mostly of people I met: Dore, a pretty girl in Hamburg, some Swiss students on the Rhine, a professor and his wife in Heidelburg and a family friend I stayed with in Karlsruhe. Also I bought about a hundred postcards and a travel poster for my German teacher. Mr. Gillem would be proud.

David's travel piece differs from most others because it focuses on an encounter with just one person. Notice, too, that the trip changed David in only a small way. He now thinks differently about taking photographs. This is a modest change and is far more credible than the grandiose claims made in countless college essays about how a summer trip transformed a student's life.

Unless you can make your travel story magical, store it in your scrapbook. Because some admissions counselors think that applicants who choose to tell about their travels are not pushing themselves creatively or intellectually, be sure you've found a fresh approach to your What-I-Did-Last-Summer essay. Don't turn an unforgettable summer adventure into a forgettable essay. For example, Tim C, an applicant to the University of Rochester, went traveling to New England and Canada, but his essay went nowhere, as this opening paragraph shows:

> An experience that has had a great meaning for me occurred the summer of my junior year. During that summer I spent a week in Maine, a week in Vermont, and a week in New Hampshire. I also visited Quebec for a briefer period of time. My trip away from home led me to mature and to obtain a better and broader picture of how other people live.

If Tim had left blank spaces where he wrote Maine, Vermont, and New Hampshire, you could fill in Maryland, Virginia, and North Carolina, or, for that matter, any other state or country on earth. The result would be the same—failure to convey the uniqueness of the experience.

Harry Bauld has labeled essays that fail to stand out "the noose with which a seventeen-year-old can hang himself." Jonathan A. Henry, admissions director at the University of Maine, agrees that the "textbook response" to a question works against the applicant. "Admissions officers read hundreds of essays each year," observes Susan Wertheimer of the UVM admissions staff, "so they can get repetitive after a while." To ensure that your essay will stand out, choose your topic with care, particularly if you are disposed to writing about travel or any of the other "hot" topics, such as divorce, the environment, and violence in the schools.

Don't turn an unforgettable summer adventure into a forgettable essay.

Answering the Offbeat Question

Many colleges, hoping to draw out the uniqueness of an applicant's personality, make unusual requests on their applications. Bennington asks you to design an experiment to determine whether toads can hear, Cornell wants to know three objects that give insight into who you are, the University of Virginia wants you to name your favorite word, Holy Cross instructs you to write a letter to the person you were when your were a high school freshman, and George Washington tells you to design a monument to honor a movement, a person, a generation, or an icon.

Such questions aren't meant to catch you. They don't have correct answers. It doesn't matter at GW whether your monument commemorates King Tut or King Kong. Colleges just want to know you better and see if you can think and write. When Johns Hopkins asks you to design a college course around the music or literature that you like, they are not interested only in what you listen to or read. They'd rather hear why you are a rap fan who curls up with Kant on weekends.

An offbeat question doesn't obligate you to write an offbeat answer. Essays that seem to have been written mainly to shock the reader or attract attention "are generally off-putting and tend to hide rather than showcase a candidate's special qualities," according to William M. Shain, dean of undergraduate admission at Vanderbilt. If you are naturally creative, write a creative essay, but if creativity is not your strong suit, try sincerity. You'll never be penalized for being honest and sincere, and you can't go wrong with an answer that sounds like you and that accurately reflects your beliefs and feelings. "Above all," adds Shain, "avoid gimmicks. They almost never improve an essay." The high school hoopster who wrote his Columbia essay on a basketball did little to enhance his chances of being admitted. Nor did an Ohio Wesleyan applicant who for no apparent reason mailed in an essay attached to a coconut.

If faced with an oddball question, beware of being too cute in your response. Some years ago, when Stanford asked, "What adjective do you think would be most frequently used to describe you by those who know you best?" one jokester replied, "terse," and didn't write the essay. University officials were not amused. In contrast, they were charmed by Elissa G's answer:

Beware of being too cute. If creativity isn't your strong suit, be sincere.

It's a nice little word—"intriguing." It carries that suave nuance of smoky cafes and *Casablanca* or a James Bond movie. All of which are not exactly appropriate, since I could never imagine myself in a sleek, black evening gown, picking up a tall handsome guy in a wild, Latin nightclub only to have my romance completely spoiled by my father's kidnapping, etc. How boring. I'm not knocking the connotation though. I rather like being a dark and mysterious lady.

Yet "intriguing" is just a bit more than a connotation. It's the ability to interest people and to keep them interested. It's a slightly contagious enthusiasm that interests people—that attracts them to you, your ideas, or your activities. That is something I certainly can do. For I can help triple the size of the Debate Team, or try something new with the yearbook, or surprise a close friend with an innovative idea . . . . and with any luck, I can intrigue you.

In her first paragraph Elissa toys with the meaning of her word, but in the second she reveals its substance. Any admissions official would be "intrigued" by Elissa and want to know more about her.

Answering the Ordinary Question

An oddball essay question may inspire quirky answers but an ordinary question shouldn't tempt you to write an ordinary response. A typical question may ask, "What personal or academic experiences were particularly rewarding for you—a project, teacher, piece of writing or research, a particular course of study?" Although the question suggests that you write about school, you are free to pick any experience whatever. You may be better off, in fact, if you choose a unique personal experience. Finding your own topic demonstrates your initiative. You can also bet that most other people will play it safe and write about school. Don't run with the crowd—unless you know that you can beat them. Otherwise, take the less-traveled route. Choose a topic that is distinctly yours. (See Chapter 3 for lots of suggestions.)

> Take the less-traveled route; choose a topic that's distinctly yours.

Unusual creativity is not essential. You can bring out your best in a sober, sensitive, and sincere essay as well. Just don't get caught in the trap of dry, long-winded and empty prose, like the writer who began his self-appraisal this way:

> During one's four years in secondary school, one's education
> is centered around a number of different things that hopefully
> will be helpful in college and in the career one pursues.

Yes, the point may be understandable, but the writing is dull and impersonal. Compare it to a statement like this:

> I wonder if what I was taught in high school will help me in
> college and afterward. If not, I will be very disappointed.

At least you hear a person's voice in those words, and that's what colleges listen for.

College admissions people generally agree that the worst essays are those that summarize the writer's high school career. Nevertheless, students keep pumping out boring recitals of what they did since ninth grade. Such writers miss an opportunity to tell the college something distinctive about themselves. Their responses also suggest an inability to think deeply and to develop ideas about a single topic. Even worse, they reveal an unwillingness to take an intellectual risk, to extend themselves beyond the ordinary and mundane. Aiming to please, they submit safe, dull essays that invariably fall flat in the admissions office.

Hoping to inspire more potent writing, Oberlin tells high school seniors, "Don't be afraid to take a risk, to be original, to tell us about successful or not-so-successful experiences." Similarly, applicants to the University of Chicago are encouraged to address topics "with utter seriousness, complete fancy, or something in between." Further instructions say, "Play, analyze (don't agonize), create, compose—let us hear the result of your thinking about something that interests you, in a voice that is your own."

Humor in Your Essay

Although essays that contain gimmicks, like puns, coined words, slang, and fractured English, may attract attention among thousands of ordinary essays, your attempt to be clever may poison

> In your essay you can give your wit a workout.

your application. An ill-timed wisecrack could miss the funny bone of a weary admissions dean. This doesn't mean you should avoid humor. On the contrary: Since you have plenty of opportunity to be sober and serious in the rest of the application, in the essay you can give your wit a workout. Readers will relish something playful, satirical, or whimsical. Don't overdo it, though. Tread lightly and cautiously with jokes and sarcasm. What you and your friends may think is uproarious in the school lunchroom could fall on its face in the admissions office. Charles Cogan, an assistant director of admission at Northwestern, tells of a student who "joked that he would kill himself if we didn't admit him. That wasn't funny. He didn't understand the concept of boundaries." Test your humor on an impartial adult before you send it to a college. If you're not usually a funny person, don't try to become one on your application. David Lettermans are not made overnight.

Sometimes gentle, self-effacing humor is best. No one at Harvard, for example, objected to Lisa E's tongue-in-cheek account of why she no longer dreamed of becoming an Amazon explorer:

> I would not make a very good adventurer for two reasons: motion sickness and ignorance. I am particularly prone to seasickness—an unfortunate circumstance, since the proper way for adventurers to travel is in boats, preferably shipwrecked ones. As for ignorance, I am prone to ignorance in all areas; although in this case I am referring only to my ignorance of jungle survival tactics. I would undoubtedly perish within twenty-four hours of my arrival in the Amazon by drowning in a bog, treading on a sleeping snake, or ingesting a poisonous species of mushroom or grub. Then again, I might be stricken by some dread jungle malady or consumed for brunch by the very tribe of cannibals I had intended to study. Even worse, I might finally arrive in the Amazon only to find myself accosted by vendors of tribal nose rings and "I survived the Amazon" tee shirts.

In writing about a significant experience for the University of Pennsylvania, Joel B poked fun at his own ineptness as an outfielder in a childhood baseball game:

> The game begins. Joel stolidly assumes his usual position in right field. Anxiety dominates his emotions. He is forced to stand outside on a field on a hot and sticky day, surrounded

by clouds of swarming gnats. He fears that a ball may never be hit to him, and the only thing more fearful than that would be for a ball to be hit to him. His pet peeve on the baseball diamond is the "easy" pop fly. Joel wishes that people wouldn't include the word easy every time that phrase is used. He could be back in school demonstrating his academic prowess. Yes, school is a place where little Joel could shine! No one could hold a candle to his mastery of multiplication tables. Not to mention spelling. *There* is a field in which he could compete with the best of them.

In Sabrina E's essay for the University of Chicago you also find humor, but humor with a bite:

Before I arrived in my present high school, I attended school in Ireland. There are many differences between American and Irish education, not the least of which is the priority placed on actual teaching. Though in America scholarship comes first, in Ireland more time is spent trying to keep us on the paths of virtue than in steering us toward the paths of wisdom. Indeed, it seemed that a veritable legion of nuns was employed solely to safeguard our morals.

Whenever one of our regular teachers was absent, we were treated to one of Sister Assumpta's lectures. This latter-day saint was, by her own account, in direct communication with God. Apparently, each night as she prepared for bed, she would fall into a trance and converse with Him. This meant that whatever she told us came directly from the horse's mouth, although we were more inclined to believe that it came from the opposite end of the same animal.

Knowing that her irreverence might disqualify her at some colleges, Sabrina sent the essay anyway. She took a gamble, but for her it was worth it, since she wouldn't have wanted to attend a college where her humor wasn't appreciated.

Whether the application questions are cute, common, or challenging, all colleges have the same basic reason for asking applicants for one or more pieces of writing. As the Columbia application puts it, "Write an essay which conveys to the reader a sense of who you are." Jennifer Stein of the Connecticut College admissions staff says it another way: "The essay serves as a mechanism for getting a glimpse at the human being behind the numbers."

As you begin to think about how you'll present yourself as a person to the college of your choice, keep asking two key questions: What's unique about me, and what do I want my reader to think of me? In your answers you're sure to find the seed of an essay that will work.

Reading Your Essay

Like customers, readers are always right. Maybe you won't like what they think about your essay. Maybe they'll misunderstand your intentions. They're still right. They get what they get—it's that simple.

Even the best writers can't always predict how readers will respond to their work. That's why you should plan to show your application essay to an unbiased reader or two before you submit it to a college. Ask your readers to tell you their impressions of the writer. If their impressions coincide with what you've intended, you're likely to have written a successful essay. Connecticut College's Jennifer Stein urges students to "remember that a human being is reading their essays, not a nameless, faceless 'Board of Admissions.' Write for someone—a friend, a family member, a teacher," Stein advises, "and your essay will be more personal and interesting."

In the pages that follow you'll be privy to thoughts and reactions of a college admissions officer recorded alongside the text of four essays. Then, you'll see the final evaluation of each candidate's work.

Joyce B

If someone were to ask me to describe myself, I would have to say that I am a person of many interests. I enjoy a simple life, yet I am not afraid to try new things.

I have been fortunate enough to become exposed to a variety of life-styles at a very early age. During my travels to Europe I was able to visit Germany, Italy, and Switzerland. There, I learned about different cultures and how other people live. Watching and meeting people is one of the many things that I enjoy.

Since the age of four, I have been dancing with "Dance Capri," a countywide Italian-American folk-dancing group. My involvement in this organization has introduced me to people who are interested in some of the same things I am. We enjoy learning about our Italian heritage and pride ourselves in keeping up the folk-dancing tradition.

Along with dancing, traveling, and meeting new people, I enjoy skiing and gymnastics. I usually ski in Vermont during my vacations, but last year I had the opportunity to ski in Quebec, Canada, for a week. I have always been on gymnastics teams, during the school year and the summer, and although I never won any special honors, I enjoy competitive gymnastics meets, especially the balance beam. For me, competing with a team has taught me what working for one common cause and reaching one common goal are like.

One of the most relaxing hobbies I enjoy is cooking. When time permits, I bake and I prepare special meals for my family. I learned how to cook through various cooking courses that I took when I was younger. In high school, I could only fit one food preparation class into my program.

Fairly dull opening. Hope it gets better. Essay has three parts: many interests, simple life, and new things. One topic, in depth, would probably be better.

"exposed"? Did she live the lifestyles or just observe them? "early age"? Three? Four? Ten? I wonder what she means. What could she have learned at age three?

No more travels? Now she's into dancing. How often does she dance? A major pastime?

Ah! She likes to join groups. That's good. I wonder if she speaks Italian.

Good transition. But she's switched her focus again!

Not another topic! Athletics. Well, we can use her on the gymnastics team.

Not much new here. Pretty trite. An example could make this sound more honest.

Why were the courses special? Good grades? She seems diligent. I bet her teachers and counselors say she's a plugger.

She's been busy, all right. How much time could she have given to these jobs? I better check her list of work experiences.

What values?

Upbeat ending. But "youth faces tomorrow" isn't too interesting.

Along with this class, I enjoyed a variety of other courses in high school. However, the ones I liked the most were jewelry, Italian and history. I believe, though, that I made the most out of every course I took in high school.

Out of school, I invest a good deal of time in various part-time jobs. My work experience includes cashier and hostess work in an Italian restaurant, and my present job, which is working as a Gal Friday in an insurance office. I also baby-sit when I have the time.

High school was and still is a time of growing and maturing for me. Although working hard and getting good grades has always been my first priority, I also established and set many of the values that guide my life today. I can confidently say that in my senior year of high school I am ready to meet the challenges of college. I am ready to move on, and I see a bright future ahead of me.

Note to Admissions Committee: Joyce B's essay suggests an active, but fragmented life. Joyce skids breezily from topic to topic, to topic, suggesting just casual involvement in many areas. Yes, she's well rounded, but so are most of our applicants. I can't find anything to distinguish her from others. After reading her essay, I don't know her very well.

Her writing is essentially correct, but it's boring. Not one of her paragraphs is developed beyond presenting some general facts about herself. Too much of her essay reiterates information already stated in her application. Moreover, Joyce fails to deliver what she promises in her opening passage. Where, for one, is her "simple life?" I recommend "rejection" unless there's evidence in her file that contradicts my impression.

Chandra B

This is the fourth essay I'm writing, and it won't be any easier than any of the first three. You see, it isn't that I enjoy writing these essays, but with each one I have found out a little bit more about myself, and that is important to me. The purpose of each essay, of course, is to show that I have a sense of who I am, but there is always more to be found at the bottom of the well called "me." I wouldn't be fooling you or anyone if I said I know absolutely, totally everything there is to know about me.

My mother said to me this evening, as she finished reading my third essay, "You know what theme I find recurrent in each of these, Chandra? A sense of struggle, of some sort of tension within you. And that, I think, is what drives you. It is helping you in your maturation. Perhaps it needs resolving, but at the same time you know it is there, and you are dealing with it."

I think that for everyone sooner or later there is a time of inner tension and struggle—a time when one asks, "Who am I? What do I mean to myself?" It is those who face this struggle and deal with it rather than deny it, who eventually succeed in being who they want to be. One must learn to make choices about what one wants to stand for, to do with one's life, and at the same time one must learn to change oneself in order to achieve this.

My first essay dealt with a struggle in choosing between a German heritage and a Jewish one. My choice, however, was neither one nor the other, but a compromise to accept both as being part of me, to reconcile rather than to deny. My second essay dealt with a choice I may still have to make, namely between choosing marine biology or genetics as a career. This is a choice I may never have to make, for I may discover something I want to do more than either of them. I have not limited myself to only these two choices. Yet even now, I think I would decide upon marine biology, not because I find it more interesting, for I find them both

Hmmm, a common topic—the struggle of writing an essay.

Well, this is different: The struggle has been worth it. She's learned about herself. I wonder what she's learned?

Perceptive. A good idea! We can't know ourselves completely, can we?

Hmm, a sensitive mother, but c'mon, no mother talks like that. She sounds like a psychology text. Good point, though, and the dialogue adds life.

Vague paragraph. A bit ponderous. I wonder what she's driving at.

Now I see! She's been struggling for an identity. And it hasn't been easy. Her mother was right.

Struggle to commu-
nicate? That's splen-
did! Chandra's a
deep thinker.

She seems high-
strung, a little tense.
Is that why she's
lonely? I wonder
what her teachers
say.

Ah, she's come back
to the struggle again.
Conclusion recalls her
opening. Nice way to
unify the piece.

She's convinced me. I
believe she'll win her
struggle. Strong, up-
beat ending.

equally so, but because I enjoy it more; I have more fun with it. My third essay dealt with a struggle I will always face, namely my need to communicate. I feel the need to know about others, and to have others learn about me. This is my way of sharing myself and partaking in others. My struggle is a fight against misunderstanding and loneliness. When we communicate, whether between people or nations, we understand each other. When we communicate, we bridge the gap of loneliness.

There will always be struggles within me, dilemmas I will face. I am determined to resolve these tensions. With each choice, I choose who I am, who I will become. Most importantly, though, it is I who makes these choices, not someone else. That is what self-determination is all about.

Note to Admissions Committee:

Chandra B views life as a serious undertaking. Her writing has conviction. She's not going to play her way through college or engage in foolishness. Her thoughtful—nay, philosophical—ideas attest to her maturity. She probably drives herself hard, maybe compulsively. She seems genuinely bound on a quest to find an identity.

Will she study hard in college? You bet, and will probably get A's. Will she contribute to the college? Intellectually, yes, and maybe in other ways, too. Let's accept her and several more passionate thinkers like her. I hope that her teacher and counselor recommendations confirm my impression that Chandra is a rare find.

Angela C

As far back as I can remember, I have excelled at sports. I was always the first in my kindergarten class to reach the swings during recess and the first to climb to the top of the rope during gym. However, while most six-year-old girl athletes tend to develop into "school-yard jocks," I seemed to lack that aggressive, competitive nature. I was much more content reading my book than keeping up with the boys. By the time I entered high school, I was clearly defined as a "student," not a "jock."

When I tried out for the field hockey team in ninth grade, it was merely because a good friend of mine begged me to do it with her. The idea of spending three hours every day running around a field didn't particularly appeal to me, but for a friend I'd do anything. After two weeks, my friend quit. Quitting has always been anathema to me, but in this case it never entered my mind anyway. I was having fun. Those three hours of practice were the best part of my day. I loved being outside, and being physically active. Most importantly, I loved being with my teammates. Between studying and practicing the piano, I'd spend so much time alone that my time on the field became a welcome and necessary break in my day. Also, coming home at six o'clock every evening helped me to budget my time, since I knew I only had a few hours in which to complete my assignments.

It wasn't until my sophomore year that field hockey became more important to me than just a social activity. It was still terrific fun since I loved getting to know the juniors and seniors on the team whom otherwise I would never have met. Some of them are still my closest friends. However, playing on the varsity squad was a very different experience from playing on the freshman team. I found myself missing holidays and giving up weekends to play hockey. The team now required a serious dedication and commitment, which I was willing to make since I enjoyed it so much. As my commitment became more serious, so did my attitude toward field hockey. I realized that I couldn't accept being a mediocre player.

Starts off like another "jock" essay—but very graceful. An appealing opening.

Oh, she's not a jock, after all. Smooth shift from kindergarten to ninth grade.

Well, she's a student and an athlete.

A rich paragraph! Shows Angela's loyalty to friends. Her perseverance, too. And the fun she's had.

And she has other interests, too.

She's well organized. That shows in her essay.

Good transition. This is moving right along. Angela is a serious hockey player.

She's obviously committed to the sport. Good, detailed writing.

She's a hard driver, too.

Interesting! She took on a challenge and won, and she's proud of her achievement. A good point.

Effective conclusion. She's summarizing her career and showing how she's changed. Good writing. How successful she's been! And modest, too.

What determination! I think she'll make it. She's unstoppable.

Mediocre is one of the most negative words I know. I knew in my sophomore year that, as the new player on the varsity team, I was also an average player. Traveling to Holland with my field hockey team revealed to me again my inadequacies when I saw the skill of some of the Europeans. Since then, by attending camps and clinics and playing in summer leagues, I've really worked hard to become a good player. I always want to be good—if not the best—at everything to which I set my mind. To be a good student comes naturally to me, but for me to be a good field hockey player requires work.

I remember when I first started playing field hockey. I thought that to be an all-county player and captain of the varsity was to be the best. Well, I *am* an all-county player and I *am* the captain of the team but one thing I am certainly not, is the best. Whenever I achieve one of my many goals, it always seems as if a new one appears ahead of me. Now that I'm a good high school player, I'm ready to start at the bottom again and work to become a good college player.

Note to Admissions Committee:

Angela C clearly demonstrates self-confidence and an upbeat personality. She's good at everything, and she enjoys all she does. Her essay indicates that she's loyal, well-organized, determined, committed to success, industrious, and fun-loving. Yet, she doesn't bowl you over with her attributes. Instead, she casually tosses them into the story of her growth as a field hockey player. In spite of all her virtues, she neither brags nor sounds like a Boy Scout. She's an all-round scholar-athlete.

Angela can write! There's not an ill-chosen word or awkward phrase in the piece. Could she have received help? Look for confirmation of writing talent in her grades and references.

My recommendation: If she's really as good as she sounds, offer her the dean's house and a Ferrari!

Eric H

It is Friday afternoon, a time I can so vividly remember enjoying. School would let out, and no matter how much homework I had, I could always relax Friday and Saturday. Unfortunately, T.G.I.F. has evolved into O.S.I.F. (Oh @#$%, it's Friday!).

A catchy opening.

Joint custody: an American revolution. Friday is the transition day, the day that a week's worth of subsistence materials have to be transported from one parent's abode to the other's. My room at Dad's has to be cleaned, my clothes washed and pressed, and other essentials placed in order. Then my odyssey commences. Somehow, I have to get all of my belongings from one end of town to the other.

Oh, another essay on divorce.

"subsistence materials" Ugh! Does he mean toothpaste, underwear, a week's supply of socks?"

"abode," "commences" Too fancy.

Usually, Mom picks me up. She tries to be tolerant but at times loses her cool. "I'm only going to do this once. If you forget anything, that's your tough luck." I try to explain that I can't fit everything I own into her Toyota. Sometimes she forgets that I didn't ask for this asinine way of life. In any event, four trips to the car later, we leave home and head for home.

Mother sounds like an ogre, probably the villain in this story.

"asinine" Good word. Eric sounds bitter.

Ah, a good line. Sardonic humor.

By the time I'm really settled, another week has passed. O.S.I.F.!, and I find myself out of breath exactly where I started. In the span of two weeks I have accomplished nothing except total aggravation. I can't even blink for fear that another Friday will come.

I don't get the point of all this. Does he mean that his life is a treadmill? Why doesn't he say so?

Like anything else, joint custody has its bright side. When my parents were divorced, Dad had a big decision to make: pack up and forget his little brats or remain for the duration. Even though he's never been nominated for any Best Daddy awards, he hasn't regretted his decision to stay.

Ah, good. There's a bright side to the story.

Well, Dad's no hero either.

The entire ordeal has brought us a world closer. When we were quite suddenly hurled into an unamiable apartment without Mom, we shared a common interest: survival. Neither of us knew how to break an egg, sew a hem, or clean a toilet bowl.

He refused to learn these things, so I had to. Today, six years later, I cook all the meals, do all the shopping, and make most of the household decisions in place of my father. He basically grants me a generous expense account of forty dollars on Friday night,

Shows maturity and responsibility, I guess.

Forty dollars? Only forty dollars? that's hard to swallow!

Puzzling. Didn't he grow close to his father? Something's missing here.

and it is up to me to see that food is purchased for the week. This burden has done wonders for my character. Many of my friends fear life at college, but not I. If I can tolerate life with my father, campus life will undoubtedly be a breeze.

Well, good. He can make jokes, despite his misery.

Another advantage to joint custody is variety. Just when I get sick of the accumulated dishes, dirty laundry, and ravenous cockroaches that are a way of life at my Dad's, I can run to Mom's for a week. Come the next Friday, you can be sure that I'll be so fed up with my mother's vexatious organization and fetish for punctuality that I'll welcome cockroaches with open arms. I think that's what is meant by escapism.

Who suggested?

It has been suggested that I stop writing essays complaining about joint custody and simply leave half of my stuff at either house. It seems logical. Maybe that's the problem; it makes sense. I don't think divorce and custody were destined by the Almighty to make sense. I suppose I just have some psychological aversion to leaving fifty percent of my life unattended for a week.

Well stated

Cute ending.

All in all, I suppose joint custody isn't so bad. I'm never bored, and I'm always on my toes. Oh @#$%, I've got to run. It's Friday!

Note to Admissions Committee:

Eric H certainly has courage! He took a personal gamble by writing about an obviously painful subject. It's not that he's looking for sympathy, but rather he chose to vent his anger about being shuttled between his parents each week. He has a right to be bitter, but I question his judgment in using the application essay as a place to blow off steam.

The essay is meant to be humorous, and it is—to a point. The humor is a thin disguise, though, for someone who laughs to hide his tears. My guess is that Eric's anguish makes him hard to like, but I'd like to know what his counselor and teachers think.

He's not a bad writer, but he seems to flaunt his vocabulary—not always successfully—perhaps thinking that college people will be impressed. His work lacks polish, but I think that in time it will improve.

His essay works neither for nor against his candidacy. My recommendation will be based on the other information in his application and file.

3 WHAT TO WRITE ABOUT

The essay instructions on the Barnard application read, in part:

> The members of the Committee on Admissions seek to gain an understanding of you as a person. This essay is your opportunity to discuss an idea that matters to you, to write about a person who has influenced you, or to describe an experience that has helped shape who you are.

As a Barnard hopeful, you probably wouldn't decline this "opportunity" to portray yourself in writing. Before you began, however, you'd probably consider more than one essay idea before settling on the one you actually use. Some writers seem to find inspired topics all around them. Others think long and deeply before writing a word. Still others arrive at their topics only after committing words to paper. To prime their creative pumps, they just start writing. Ideas start to flow, and suddenly they discover what they want to write about. (If you're one of those people who often suffers from a shortage of writing ideas, turn to the end of this chapter for a few thoughts on how to tap into a good source of material, namely, your own mind.)

To find a topic for yourself, use whatever method suits you, but stay ever mindful of the intent of your essay—to project personal qualities not readily apparent in other places.

You may think of the essay as a burden, but colleges regard it as an opportunity for you to put the finishing touch on your application, as your last chance to amplify or add information about your background, experience, talent, skills, character, personal philosophy, and zest for life.

How do you do all that in an essay of 250 to 500 words? The Bennington application recognizes the challenge and simply comments, "We hope that the process of writing these essays gives you a chance to discover something about who you are and what you want from college. Questions like these are much too interesting to have any easy, final, or correct answers. So relax. Take some risks. Surprise yourself."

The Topics

Colleges have devised innumerable topics. Some applications offer a choice, and others tell you to write whatever you please—as though to test your inventiveness. Still others lay out specific guidelines for an essay, partly to see whether you can follow directions. Several colleges suggest topics but also offer you a chance to make up one of your own.

Although application essay questions differ in detail from one college to the next, most of them fall loosely into five groups, each with opportunities to project yourself onto paper, but each with perils to watch out for: (1) Why go to college, and why here? (2) Who are you? (3) Would you tell us a story about yourself? (4) What is important to you? and (5) What would you like to tell us about yourself?

Responses to these questions frequently overlap. If, for instance, you were to write on a *significant personal experience*— one of the most popular topics—you'd probably tell a story. The experience you choose would also reveal who you are, and your explanation of its significance would identify some of your personal values.

In the sample questions and topics listed in this chapter, you may not find the exact question your college asks but you'll probably recognize one that comes close.

Why Go to College? Why Here?

From questions about your plans for the future, colleges hope to discern your route for the next four years. What will the college experience mean to you? Will you study, or will you party? Have you thought about why you're going to college at all? Expecting a look at your educational map, colleges often make inquiries such as these:

—Why do you want to go to college?
—Why do you want to go to this college, in particular?
—What are your career objectives, and how will college help you achieve them?
—How will this college help you fulfill your goals and aspirations?
—What will your presence add to this college?

No one answer to such questions is preferable to another. If you aim to be a dentist or a Washington lawyer, that's fine. Yet no college seeks to fill its classrooms with only one type of student. In the main, colleges try to keep their enrollments balanced. It's not a weakness, therefore, to admit that you don't know how you want to spend the rest of your life. College is for exploring. In fact, liberal arts students frequently come to campuses with receptive and open minds. More than likely, they'll rummage through many of the offerings on which a college has built its reputation.

As you explain your intentions to a college, consider these essay-writing hints:

DO . . .

✓ Answer the question being asked, not the one you'd like to answer.

✓ Before writing a word, scrutinize the college's offerings. If you expect to major in, say, ecology, be sure the college has an environmental studies program.

✓ Think hard about what *you* hope to get out of college, avoiding clichés, such as "I want an education," "I want to get a good, well-paying job," and "I want to be a success in my chosen field."

✓ Try to figure out why this college appeals to you. Did the college representatives make it sound exciting? Did you visit the campus and get good vibes? Is there a particular program that has attracted your interest?

✓ Focus on educational or personal reasons for going to college, not on social, economic, or family reasons.

DON'T . . .

✗ Don't use flattery. All colleges already know how good they are.

✗ Don't stress that you love the college's location, size, or appearance. By applying there, you have implied that those characteristics are acceptable to you.

✗ Don't tell a college that it's your "safe" school.

✗ Don't write that you're going to college because you don't know what else to do.

Finally, don't take any of these precautions as the last word in application essay writing. Use them at your discretion. Don't ignore them, though, unless you have a sound reason for doing so. Jim D, for example, came right out and told Bowdoin he wanted to go there precisely because of its location. "Like Thoreau," Jim wrote, "I feel most alive near wild streams and forests."

Answers That Worked

Marian T's afterschool work in a fabric shop inspired her love of fashion and developed her flair for design. "In college," Marian wrote, "I plan to major in fine arts."

David B studied four languages in high school. Because of his bent toward languages and foreign cultures, he wants a career in international affairs as a businessman or diplomat, but he said, "A stint in the Peace Corps will come first."

Lisa C loves to read. "I can't imagine a career more suited to me than librarian in a school or a public library," she wrote.

Wendy W has wide and wandering interests. Last year it was dance, this year it is community service. Wendy thinks of college as a place for "accumulating more interests, for meeting people, for working hard, and, ultimately, for finding a niche in life to fill."

Andy S has always taken the hardest courses. He doesn't know why, except that doing well in tough courses has made him feel good. "I hope to continue feeling good in college," he quipped.

Deena R admires one of her high school English teachers. Since he's told her wonderful stories of Williams College, she'd like to go there, too. "I plan to major in English," she wrote, "and find out if Mr. Stern's stories are true."

Karen S's "most joyful and gratifying high school experience" has been working with mentally retarded children. In college she'll major in special education.

Mark D lost his father and a brother last year. Yet he has retained his essential optimism. He wrote that "there is still a promise in life for me. There are so many things that I have not yet experienced, but inevitably must." That's why he wants to go to college.

Don Z has met many people through playing guitar at festivals and nightspots. He thrives on people whose style of living differs from his. Don asked, "What better place than a giant university is there for finding a variety of people?"

Becky B is thinking of a career in acting. She expects a college education to help her become a more complete person. "My wish," she wrote, "is not only to be a good actor but also a good person, and my belief is that they might be the same thing."

Who Are You?

Colleges have heard what others think of you—teachers, counselors, interviewers. With self-assessment questions, they hope to learn what you think of yourself. Do you know who you are? Are you aware of how others react to you? Would you like to change in some way? Self-knowledge is often thought to be a prerequisite for understanding the world, and an essay that demonstrates that you know yourself will give your application a big boost. To check the depth of your insight, colleges ask questions like these:

—What is important to you?
—How would you describe yourself as a human being?
—How might a freshman roommate describe you?
—Write your own recommendation to college.

—If you could strengthen one aspect of yourself, what would it be? Why?

—What quality do you like best in yourself? What quality do you like least?

—Imagine yourself as a book or other object. How would people react to you?

—What makes you different from other people?

In your response, readers hope to find clues to your personality. Unless you present yourself as a bizarre monster, they won't necessarily care whether you are soft-spoken or loud, a realist or a dreamer, a liberal or a rock-hard conservative. They'll give you short shrift, however, if they think you are a fake. Above all, then, in writing "who are you?" essays, be truthful with yourself—as truthful as you've ever been before.

> Telling the truth doesn't mean you must bare your soul.

Telling the truth doesn't mean you must bare your soul and disclose your deepest secrets. Colleges don't need to know about your sex life, psychiatric treatment, or drug and drinking problems. On the other hand, you needn't portray yourself as a saint. Students have written successful essays about their cynicism, frustration, greed, and favorite vices. "Every year," says Barbara Jan Wilson, formerly the dean of admission at Wesleyan and now a university vice president, "we get an essay or two about a student's first sexual experience, written as a literal response to the 'significant experience' question." Wilson says, "Don't do this. It shows poor judgment and is not relevant to admission to college." In the end, let good taste govern your choice of material. If you have doubts, switch topics. Jenny G wrote an essay about a family drug problem, thought the better of it afterward, and wrote another, highlighting her good judgment.

DO . . .

✓ Answer the question that is asked.

✓ Be as honest as you can. Search for qualities you really have, not those you wish for.

✓ Emphasize specific, observable qualities that show your distinctive personality. Imagine that your reader will someday have to pick you out in a crowd.

✓ Illustrate your qualities with specific examples. Use telling anecdotes to support your opinions of yourself.

✓ Ask people who know you well whether they agree with your self-analysis.

DON'T . . .

✗ Don't be evasive. Stand up for what you think about yourself.

✗ Don't be too cute or coy. Sincerity is preferable.

✗ Don't choose a characteristic merely to impress the college.

✗ Don't write everything you know about yourself. Focus on one or two of your outstanding qualities.

✗ Don't write an essay fit for *True Confessions*.

Remember that you can violate every rule and still write a compelling essay. Just be aware of the perils.

Answers That Worked

Suzannah R thinks of herself as a dynamo in danger of burning out by age twenty. She can't control her energy level. She's impatient and often intolerant of others' laid-back attitudes. She added, "As I have grown older, I feel I am learning to accept other people's shortcomings."

David V said, "The most important fact to know about me is that I am a Black person in a White society." David considers himself an outsider and expects to continue feeling alienated as long as racial prejudice exists.

Ellen E contrasted her goofing off early in high school ("personal problems and just plain stupidity") with her productive junior and senior years. In effect, she was reborn during the summer between tenth and eleventh grades.

Allison R has fought shyness all her life. She recounted three moments in her life when shyness defeated her. In contrast, she told of three recent incidents that have helped to raise her self-esteem.

Steve M sees himself as a latter-day Clarence Darrow, always standing in defense of the little guy, often taking the minority point of view in class just to generate a little controversy. If others consider him obnoxious, he claimed, "it's a small price to pay for a life full of heated debates and discussions."

———————

Adam L works 25 to 30 hours a week during the school year loading and unloading trucks for the family business. He says that working such long hours "means I don't get to 'live' as much." But he takes solace in thinking that he knows the value of hard work and when he graduates from college, he'll be better prepared for the real world.

———————

John K sees himself as a character in a movie. When he's alone he pretends he's Leonardo DiCaprio, playing the role of a Generation-X bachelor. He even hums background film music when he's driving and jogging.

———————

Brendan B is a gourmet cook. He loves to eat. "You are what you eat," he believes, so he defined himself by the food he enjoys most. From meat and potatoes, for example, he has gained a strong will. From French sauces, he has derived a subtle sense of humor.

———————

Nicole W is a perfectionist. From schoolwork to keeping her room in order, she cannot allow herself to do anything shabbily or incomplete. She is worried about "getting a slob for a college roommate."

———————

Dena P, a gymnast since age eight, works like a demon to be number one. Ever striving for perfection, she wrote, "I know now that when it comes to making commitments, I can be ready to make them."

———————

Doug M is an adopted Korean orphan. He sees himself as a child of two cultures. Although a double identity causes confusion in others, he feels "more fortunate and richer" than his American classmates.

Jennifer B loves computers. Everything about computers comes so easily and naturally to her that she said, "I sometimes think that I must have been born in an Apple Computer factory. Instead of brains, maybe I have memory boards and microcircuitry inside my head."

Would You Tell Us a Story About Yourself?

Telling stories is a most natural thing to do. When you come home from school you tell what happened that day. You tell friends what Donna said to Fred and how Kathy felt afterward.

The story you write for a college application isn't expected to be like a superbly crafted tale by Poe or O'Henry, just an autobiographical account of an experience. It should tell about something that happened and what it meant to you. A good story both entertains and informs the reader. A story written for a college does even more. It suggests your values, clarifies your attitudes, and, better yet, breathes life into your personality.

Although storytelling possibilities are limitless, application questions usually direct you to identify and discuss a noteworthy time in your life:

—Write about a significant experience or event in your life and what it meant to you.

—Write an original essay about a humorous personal experience.

—What is it that you have done that best reflects your personality?

—Describe a challenging situation and how you responded.

—Comment on an experience that helped you discern or define a value you hold.

—What is the most difficult thing you've ever done?

—Write about a group endeavor in which you participated, and describe your contribution.

In response to any of these topics, you can write a story about last night or pick an event from the time you were a small child. The experience can have been instantaneous or long-lived, a once-in-a-lifetime occasion or a daily occurrence. It can have taken place in a schoolroom, a ballroom, a mountaintop—anywhere, in fact, including inside your head.

An event need not have been earthshaking to inspire a story. Almost everything you do from the moment you wake up holds possibilities.

> Almost anything you do from the moment you wake up has possibilities.

If you haven't noticed how life is crammed with moments of drama, cast off those blurry lenses and start to look for the hidden realities behind the daily face of things: In a disagreement with your brother, in an encounter with a former girlfriend or boyfriend, or in a teacher's criticism you may find the ingredients for an insightful, dramatic essay. Simply by making a list of ten things that happened yesterday and another ten things that occurred last week, you may trigger more than one essay idea.

If you want to write about the time you made headlines, that's great, but most people lead ordinary lives. To take a common experience and interpret it as only you can is a perfectly acceptable way to think about the task before you.

DO . . .

- ✓ Answer the question that is asked.
- ✓ Choose an experience you remember well. Details will make or break your story.
- ✓ Pick an experience you can dramatize. Let the reader hear people speaking and see people acting!
- ✓ Focus on a specific incident or event.
- ✓ Make yourself the central character in the story.

DON'T . . .

✗ Don't think that a commonplace event can't be turned into an uncommonly good story.

✗ Don't choose a complicated event unless you can explain it briefly. Fill in background, but focus on what happened.

✗ Don't lie. If you must fabricate material for effect, be sure it sounds like the truth.

✗ Don't ramble. Rambling stories are boring.

✗ Don't explain your point with a lecture on what the reader is supposed to notice. Let the story make its own point.

Answers That Worked

Ted B collects things: Matchbox cars, license plates, matchbook covers, and rocks. From his hobby he has learned about design, geography, advertising, and geology—and interior decorating, too, for after five years of collecting, he literally wallpapered the foyer of his house with matchbook covers.

Pete S was riding in a car with his brother. At a stoplight a pretty girl in a neighboring car smiled at him. Pete looked away. Afterward, he berated himself and resolved to become more outgoing and more responsive to others.

Colin V is Catholic. Last year on May 6th his Jewish godson was born. As a result, Colin's eyes have been opened to the world of Jewish customs. "I look at everything differently now," Colin wrote.

Jenny B's hard-of-hearing grandfather lives with the family. Whenever Jenny tries to help the old man, he rebuffs her. A blowup occurred after Jenny knocked too loudly on his door to summon him to the phone. The incident has caused her to reflect at length on the needs of the aged.

Mary G, from a middle-class family, works in a slum area soup kitchen with her church group. She'll never be a social reformer, but the work, she claims, has made her "more sensitive to the needs of the poor and homeless."

Roy O's summer at a lake with his father building a cabin gave him time to think about how lucky he was to have been born in the United States into a fairly well-to-do family. "I'll never take the blessings of life for granted again," he wrote.

Liz H and her twin sister Mary have rarely been apart. Lately, Liz has found it necessary to seek her own identity and has taken up running as a way to get away. Her hours of solitude on the road have helped to strengthen the bonds with her sister.

Sandy M says, "Sunday is always spent gathering the scattered fragments of my life." It's the day she uses to catch up on schoolwork, gain some perspective on her social life, make peace with her parents, and look in the mirror for a long time trying to figure out who she is.

Lauren S has always been plagued by insecurity. An offhand remark by an art teacher ("Hey, you're good!") has helped her to build confidence and work that much harder in her courses. She's beginning to see signs of how good she really is.

Lisa R's parents were divorced. The complex legal negotiations that accompanied the split, while painful to her, so fascinated Lisa that she plans to become a lawyer.

Robert S thinks that he has been ostracized at his school because of his ragged appearance. Instead of wearing a jacket and tie to an honor society interview, he showed up in a black leather jacket and torn jeans. The incident heightened his awareness that people are judged by superficialities, not by their character.

What Is Important to You?

Would you rather hear a Bach cantata or a Phish album? Would you prefer to go bowling or spend an afternoon in an art museum? Do you like fast foods or nouvelle cuisine? To a great extent, your preferences define you. Hoping for a glimpse of your taste and your biases, many colleges ask you to write a "choice" essay. Rather than give you a menu of choices, however, they tell you to come up with one of your own—your favorite quotation, an influential person in your life, a significant book you've read:

> —What is your favorite quotation? Explain your choice.
> —What have you read that has had special significance for you? Explain.
> —Identify a person who has had a significant influence on you, and describe that influence.
> —Tell us about a personal, local, national, or international issue of particular concern to you.
> —What is your favorite noun? What does it mean to you?
> —If you could invent anything, what would you create? Discuss.
> —If you could affect the outcome of human history by changing a particular event, what event would you choose? How would you change it, and why?
> —If you could spend an evening with any prominent person—living, deceased, or fictional—whom would you choose, and why?

What you choose when responding to such questions is important. But the rationale for your choice is even more important and should make up the heart of your essay.

The key to writing a forceful response is that your choice has some direct, personal bearing on your life. A quotation from Shakespeare may sound impressive, but if you pick it only for effect, you'd be better off with a lyric from Lyle Lovett or a maxim of your grandmother's. Before you select an important world issue like terrorism or overpopulation, be sure you've been personally touched by it. Instead of condemning war, tell what you've done to support peace. If you write on a book, don't limit yourself to school reading. What you've read on your own tells far more about you than any class assignment.

If you are wavering between two equally good choices, tip your scales toward less popular subjects. Conversations with Columbus, George Washington, and Princess Diana have already been written. So have numerous essays about cures for cancer and AIDS. Many students have already written about altering human history by eliminating war, preventing the birth of Hitler, and canceling Lincoln's evening at Ford's Theater. They also have expressed concerns about affirmative action, nuclear power, abortion, capital punishment, poor people, and gay rights. Countless others have been influenced by a grandparent, a sibling with a handicap, a teacher, or a virtuous public figure.

Nevertheless, the last word on all these subjects hasn't yet been written. Although admissions staffers may frown on still more essays about peace or pollution, they'll welcome any essay that's genuine, insightful, and interesting.

DO . . .

- ✓ Answer the question that is asked.
- ✓ Choose a subject that you care about.
- ✓ Let your head and heart be your source of material.
- ✓ Think of at least three very good personal reasons for your choice.
- ✓ Try out more than one answer. Submit the one that you like best.

DON'T . . .

- ✗ Don't choose a topic merely to look good.
- ✗ Don't be self-conscious about your choice. Just tell the truth.
- ✗ Don't choose a subject that requires research. Let your experience guide you.

Lisa D, born in South Africa, came to the United States at age eleven. Her essay recalls her black nurse, who was forbidden to enter the park where Lisa and her friends played hopscotch and tag.

Sabrina S is the drum major of her school's marching band. She recalls a time when she thought that winning competitions was the band's only purpose. As a senior, she realizes that there's more to it than collecting trophies. The band has become an essential part of her life. "The school parking lot became my 'home' and the members of the band have become my 'family,'" she wrote.

Barbara B has been fascinated with space flight ever since second grade when the elementary school librarian introduced her to a science fiction book, *Matthew Looney, the Boy from the Moon.* In college Barbara expects to major in physics and then become an astronaut.

Luke J chose the word *family* as his favorite noun. To explain, he wrote a moving portrait of a close-knit family. Five times in the last ten years the family has moved. Luke's father works overseas for months at a time. Yet, Luke derives stability from his family, despite its fragmented lifestyle.

Robert B refuted the old adage, "You can't compare apples and oranges," by writing a tongue-in-cheek comparison of the two fruits. As a result, he wonders about the validity of other pieces of wisdom. He plans to research next "You can't tell a book by its cover" and "Absence makes the heart grow fonder."

Carl G, who has a deaf younger brother, wrote about *Dancing without Music—Deafness in America,* a book that persuaded him and his parents to introduce young Danny to other deaf people as a way to help the boy find an identity as a hearing-impaired person.

Gary K wrote about Steven, his mentally retarded brother. All his life, Gary has been Steven's fun committee, psychiatrist-at-home, and teacher. Gary wept recently after he found Steven eating pineapple from a can. It had taken Gary six weeks to teach Steven how to use a can opener.

―――――――――

Jordana S said that her favorite cartoon character, Linus from "Peanuts," has qualities that she envies: stability, self-confidence, and grace under pressure. As for his security blanket, "Linus carries it to show that he's secure enough not to worry what others think about his carrying it."

―――――――――

Joanna L named Miss B, her elementary school gym teacher, as a significant person in her life. Miss B so intimidated Joanna that "even today the smell of a gymnasium and the sight of orange mats stimulate feelings of terror and dread."

―――――――――

What Would You Like to Tell Us About Yourself?

Perhaps the toughest writing assignment is the one without a suggested topic:

—We would welcome any comments you care to make about yourself.
—The essay is an important part of your application. It will help admissions officers gain a more complete picture of you. Use the essay to tell about yourself.
—If there is anything else you would like to tell us about you, please explain on an additional sheet.
—Please use this page to give us any information you think would be helpful to us as we consider your application.
—The purpose of this application is to help us learn about you.
—Is there additional information we should know that will help us to make an informed decision?
—To better understand you, what else should we know?

Without restrictions, you may literally send in anything. Starting from scratch, you can cook up a totally new piece of writing. Or you may submit a poem, a story, or a paper you've written for school or yourself. Applicants who have written for publications often send samples of their writing. If you include a previously written piece, don't just pull it from your files and throw it in the envelope. Carefully explain on a new cover page what it is and why you chose it.

A word of caution: Unless you are using the Common Application, avoid submitting a reheated essay, one you've written for another application. A college that asks you to write on a book that has left an impact on you won't appreciate an essay entitled "My Job in the Day Care Center." Naturally, you may be able to incorporate bits and pieces from all your other college essays, but rework your material, disguise it, change its focus to the question you are answering. In a pinch, you may of course need to send the same essay to two or more colleges. Should your essay be so good that you feel compelled to use it again, do so, but courteously tell the second or third college what you have done and why. Your honesty will be appreciated.

> Avoid submitting a reheated essay, one you've written for another application.

Ignore all the foregoing advice if you're submitting the Common Application. A college that accepts the Common Application expects you to write only one essay, which you may duplicate and send to every college in the consortium.

DO . . .

- ✓ Pick something important—something that matters to you.
- ✓ Consider explaining anything unusual that has influenced your school or home life.
- ✓ Use a style of writing that sounds like you.
- ✓ Write the sort of piece (for example, essay, poem, internal monologue) that you've written successfully in the past.

DON'T . . .

✗ Don't turn down the college's invitation to write more about yourself.

✗ Don't put on airs to try to impress the college. Be yourself.

✗ Don't repeat what you've written elsewhere on your application.

✗ Don't try to use a form or style of writing for the first time unless you have a record of successful writing experiments.

✗ Don't write the essay (or any other part of your application) the night before it's due.

Answers That Worked

Bonnie W asserted that writing the college essay helped her sort out her feelings about herself. She has finally accepted the fact that she is a nonconformist. "I used to run with the 'in' crowd," she wrote, "but now I don't give a damn. I can breathe."

———————

Lillian S, a student of karate, wrote about how it feels to break a board with her bare hand. Writing about karate, she said, has heightened her concentration as she trains to earn a black belt.

———————

Dave E reflected on violence in America. His thoughts had been triggered by a triple murder that had occurred a few weeks earlier in a neighboring town.

———————

Kevin B wrote a funny piece on being a motorcycle enthusiast. On a recent trip to Massachusetts with the school band, his overnight host expected him to come equipped with a switchblade and chains. The folks in the Bay State seemed disappointed by his "normal" behavior and appearance.

———————

Jenny J wrote a collection of fables, each concluding with a moral or maxim to illustrate a strongly held conviction. One story ended, "Be satisfied with who you are." Another, "Don't turn your back on anyone in pursuit of power."

Adam B wrote a piece detailing the first time he baked walnut tarts. Like an expectant father, he paced the kitchen floor, waiting for the oven bell to sound. At the gong, his whole family rushed in for a taste. The verdict? "Well, that night I retired with a grin on my face," wrote Adam.

Ray G, a high school baseball player, wrote a tongue-in-cheek analysis of his statistics. Last season he batted .300. He also got 600 on his math SAT I. "Does that mean my math is twice as good as my hitting?" Ray asked. "I doubt that my math teacher would say so," he added.

Jodi F wrote about a family trip to Europe. Her parents were on the verge of separation, but during the tour of Italy, France, and Spain her mother and father made peace. "How odd," thought Jodi, "to save my home by leaving it."

Barry G wrote of waking in the middle of a hot summer night and going to the roof of his apartment building for some air. Peering at the lights below, he experienced a self-revelation. As an intelligent person, he realized that if he set his mind to it, he could do almost anything he wanted to with his life. Thinking of possibilities, he stayed on the roof until dawn.

Pamela M reviewed her dancing career since age four and concluded by stating, "Dancing has allowed me to express myself from within and to be, feel, and love who I am."

Thinking of Ideas to Write About

If you're one of those blessed writers who explode with ideas for every assignment, read no further. You don't need this section. If, however, you routinely come back empty handed from topic searches, try some of these popular do-it-yourself techniques for spawning ideas:

1. If your essay due date is weeks or months away, start a journal today. Innumerable college essays have begun life as journal entries. From now on, record whatever catches your eye or tickles your brain. Anything! Since no one else will see what you write, literally everything is OK. Some of what you write may be silly and pointless, but not if you force yourself to tell the truth and only the truth.

   Frankly, your honest images and thoughts may lead to a dead end, but journal keepers often run into rich veins of ideas in their daily entries. After a few days, a journal begins to be a source book of information on you. When you need a topic for your college essay, you'll have a personal reference book at your fingertips. In its pages you may discover the stuff to write the essay of your life.

2. Try free-writing. That is, write nonstop for ten to fifteen minutes a day, paying no heed to grammar, spelling, or punctuation. Concentrate on telling the truth about whatever is on your mind that day. You'll be amazed at how rapidly ideas flow when you write unself-consciously and without preplanning. After free-writing you won't have a polished essay, or even a first draft, but you might have bagged one or two surprisingly fertile ideas.

3. Focus your free-writing. Once you have done some free-writing, reread what you've written. Circle any idea or phrase you like or that holds promise for an essay topic. Take one of the ideas that feels right, and free-write on that one. When you focus your free-writing, you accumulate possibilities on a topic. The human mind spits out thoughts so speedily that most of them vanish before they reach consciousness. In free-writing, though, you can preserve thoughts before they get away. Try focused free-writing again and again, until you've arrived at a satisfactory essay topic.

4. Like pulling out a stopper, making a list often starts the flow of ideas. A list of items, quickly jotted down, may bring to mind just the topic you're looking for. Writing down lists of influential people in your life or books you've read acts like a simple word-

association exercise. As your mind makes connections, one name calls up memories of the next and the next. Anything and anyone can go on your list. At first, don't be particular. Later you can start to be discriminating as you narrow the choices for a possible essay topic.

5. On a very long sheet of paper—perhaps several pieces of attached computer paper—create a timeline of your life. Write down every event you can think of, whether you think it's important or not. Ask people whom you've known for a long time to suggest additional items for your time line. A perusal of the finished work may suggest lifelong themes, key events, and personal interests that can be turned into essay topics.

6. Talk to anyone who'll listen—a teacher or coach, a boss or a soulmate also in search of a topic. When you least expect it, one of you might just blurt out the very idea you've been looking for. Besides, when you solve a problem with someone else, you often get a bonus called synergism—the combined power of two heads working together, which usually exceeds the total power of two heads working separately.

4 COMPOSING *YOUR* ESSAY

You probably won't get out of high school without writing some sort of essay on *Macbeth,* or if not *Macbeth,* then on the Great Depression or dissecting a frog. By this time in your life, in fact, you've probably written enough essays to fill a large book. When writing those essays, perhaps you sat down, spilled your thoughts onto the page, and handed in your paper. Maybe you wrote a rough draft and went back later to reorganize and rephrase your ideas. Possibly, you thought out ahead of time what you wanted to say and prepared a list of ideas or an outline. Maybe you used a combination of methods, varying them from time to time according to the importance of the essay.

Everyone who writes uses a process of some kind. Some processes seem to work better than others. The variations are endless, however, and the actual process you use is as personal and unique as your fingerprints. Since it is personal, let me step out of my role as writing instructor for a moment and describe the process I used to write this chapter so far.

Before I typed a word, I had a general idea of what I wanted to say: namely, that anyone facing an essay question on a college application has already had plenty of writing experience and that the same process a person used to write essays in school can be used to write an essay for college. Furthermore, I wanted to assure the reader that no single process is better than any other, as long as it works. With those thoughts floating around in my head, I started to write, hoping that one idea would flow smoothly into the next. I also hoped that extraneous ideas wouldn't lead me away from what I had in mind, something that frequently happens when I write.

> The process you use to write is as personal and unique as your fingerprints.

Fairly rapidly for me, because I'm usually a very slow writer, I typed the first two paragraphs. Then I reread them. Luckily, they seemed to stick to the topic and they more or less expressed my thoughts. I wasn't altogether happy with my opening sentence, however, which originally read, "By this time in your life you must have written a ream of essays." I thought that some of my readers wouldn't know the word *ream,* so I changed the sentence to one that would surely evoke an image of a lot of pages: "By this time in your life you must have written enough essays to fill a large book."

A moment later, however, I decided that even that sentence wasn't right for an opening. I needed an idea that hit closer to my readers' experience. So I inserted two new sentences, turning my original first sentence into the third. Still later, I added the phrase "in fact" to that sentence, intending to bind the thoughts in the first three sentences more closely to each other.

As you see, I like to write a few paragraphs as quickly as I can, then return to them before going on. I don't always do that, however. Sometimes I write more, sometimes less, before doubling back to rewrite and edit. Other writers work differently, and so, no doubt, do you.

If you compare my original opening paragraphs, reproduced below, with the printed version at the start of this chapter, you'll discover several more changes, each intended to make the writing clearer and more interesting. All the while, I kept thinking of you, my reader. I figured that if you are going to spend time reading my words, the least I could do is make the time worth your while. I also wanted to make you feel compelled to read on. If the phone rang while you were reading, I was hoping you'd be annoyed at the interruption.

By this time in your life you must have written a ream of essays. In fourth grade, remember writing about "My Trip to Disney World"? More recently, perhaps, you wrote about irony in *Macbeth* or Chinese immigration to the United States. When you wrote those essays, you probably used a technique that seemed right for you. Perhaps you just sat down, spilled your thoughts onto the page, went back later, and reorganized and rephrased your ideas over and over. You may have thought out what you wanted to say ahead of time and prepared some sort of list or outline of your ideas to guide you as you wrote. You may have used a combination of methods.

Everyone who writes anything uses a process of some kind. Some processes seem to work better than others for certain writers. The variations are endless, however, and the actual process you use is personal and as unique to you as your fingerprints. Since it is so personal, let me step down from my post as giver of information about essay writing for a moment and describe the process I used to write this chapter so far.

Thinking About the Reader

You and I have made a kind of agreement. Simply by reading these words, you have agreed to let me enter your life. Thanks. My end of the bargain is harder. I have to keep writing until I'm finished, but you can stop reading at any time.

I don't want you to stop, however. So as I write, I try everything I can to hold your interest, to keep your mind and eyes fastened to these words. That's a tough assignment. Since you're a stranger to me, I don't know what you'll understand or what will grab you. I have to keep guessing. Even if my guess is wrong, I can't stop, can't go back and try again. If you shut this book right now, I'll never know it. No physical force in the universe is strong enough to keep one small muscle in your head from shifting your eyes away from this page. Only the compelling power of my words, along with some lucky guesswork, can do it.

As a writer of a college essay, you face a challenge similar to mine, except that you can be pretty sure your reader will stick with you to the last word. Because you have a reasonable guarantee of an audience doesn't make the job of writing any easier, however. You're still obliged to give the readers something they want to read. Writing the essay is a lot like giving a gift to a friend. You think about what your friend would like, you try to please, you choose carefully and you present the gift as stylishly as you can. If all goes well, you get a reward for your effort.

> Writing an essay is a lot like giving a gift to a friend. You try to please.

But, first, it's work.

Warming Up

Once you know the questions on your application, you're likely to start thinking about what to write. As you reach into your background to search for a subject, don't lose heart if at first you come up empty-handed. You may need a warming-up period to help you find a subject and to prime you for the vigorous mental work ahead. In fact, the ultimate quality of your essay may depend in part on your warm-ups.

For most students, the high school years rush by like a raging river. It's hard to stop and step back a moment to reflect on your life, on how far you've come and where you'd like to go. Now, on the verge of applying to college, is the right time for you to try.

Start with a personal inventory. The key word is *personal*—for your eyes only. Think of who you are and how you got that way. You might begin, for example, simply by making a list of adjectives that describe what you like about yourself. Then make another list of what you dislike. Don't worry if the second list is longer than the first—most people are pretty hard on themselves. Study these lists for patterns, inconsistencies, and unusual combinations. For instance, Gina S, whose list appears below, considers herself both "generous to others" and "self-centered." Is Gina contradicting herself? Is she being untruthful? Does she change from time to time? Since the list is personal, no one but Gina needs to know.

Gina's Personal Inventory

What I like about myself	*What I dislike*
loyal to my friends	my nose
idealistic	short temper
trusting	uncomfortable with
determined to succeed	strangers
mysterious	need a lot of sleep
ambitious	living in the past
competitive	impulsive
generous to others	lack of athletic talent
insightful about myself	can't carry a tune
sensitive to others' feelings	gluttonish
good listener	envious of friends
good memory	(sometimes)
energetic	overconsiderate of
flirtatious	others (sometimes)
	hate math
	often late for appoint-
	ments
	self-centered
	stubborn
	basically shy
	indecisive

Once you complete a list, rank the qualities in order of importance. Which quality would you be most reluctant to give up?
Which would you give up first? Which are you proudest of? Which
would you most like to change? Answers to such questions define
to respond precisely as you do.

Most items on your own personal inventory will differ from
Gina's. Yet, it shouldn't surprise you to find some similarities.
Although no item may immediately strike you as the focus of a distinctive essay, a few imaginative connections could lead you directly
to a suitable subject. Notice how Gina might have developed several
possible subjects from her inventory:

> Gina claims to be "competitive," but she also "lacks athletic
> talent." Her competitive nature, therefore, may emerge in the
> classroom instead of the gym. Perhaps she competes to win
> awards as the best reader, writer or mathematician. She may
> compete for recognition on the job or at home. Regardless of
> the place, Gina's need to excel could be the focus of her essay.
>
> Gina says she's a "glutton," presumably for food. Since a
> college doesn't necessarily need to know that, Gina could
> turn gluttony into a metaphor and focus her essay on being
> a glutton for success. Perhaps she derives satisfaction from
> being a successful student, friend or member of a particular
> group.
>
> Gina also says she's "impulsive." In a way, her "short tem-
> per" confirms that she occasionally rushes into things. On the
> other hand, she might point out that her impulsiveness gives
> her an urge to help anyone in need. Her essay might focus on
> an incident that demonstrates her unusual generosity. A brief
> discussion about becoming a social worker someday would
> add a fitting conclusion to her essay.

Ultimately, Gina found her subject in an incident that would
not have occurred unless she truly had a "good memory." This
excerpt from her essay tells what happened:

> I had just come from the elephant house at the zoo when I
> spotted Bucky, my old swimming counselor at Camp Merri-
> wood. It was six years since I saw him last. I remembered him
> only in a Princeton tee shirt and a swimsuit and never imag-
> ined that he even owned long pants and a parka, but I recog-
> nized his face instantly. I called out his name and introduced
> myself.

He looked at me and said, "Oh, I remember you, Gina," but I knew he was just being polite. To him I could have been Jenny, Margie, Eva, Ruthie, Debbie, Abby, or any one of the dozens of squealing ten-year-old girls at camp that summer.

We talked a little while about people and events at camp. No, he didn't really remember the kids on my relay team. Well yes, he only had a faint memory of the swim meet we won against Camp Harding, in which I won two races.

"What are you up to now?" he asked. When I told him I was looking for a summer job, he said his company sometimes hired high school students in the summer and that I should apply.

Gina landed a summer job in Bucky's firm doing something called "customer relations," a glamorous term for helping to keep the files straight. Gina observed in her essay, though, that she was glad to be working at all. Then she added:

I got the job as a result of having a good memory. Since then I have become more interested in memory and how it works. I have read some books on the subject and have learned some ways to improve my own memory. In less than a minute I can now memorize ten vocabulary words or the names of ten people I never met before. Elephants are not supposed to forget, which may or may not be true. However, I wonder if remembering Bucky was related to my visit to the elephants in the zoo.

Gina launched her essay with a short anecdote meant to illustrate her good memory. For every quality you list on a personal inventory, try also to think of evidence that proves that you are indeed what you claim to be. A single example is all it takes to get an essay underway.

Another place to locate essay subjects is in your answers to a set of questions such as these:

—What are you good at?
—What are you trying to get better at?
—What has been your greatest success? Your greatest failure?
—What three words would you like engraved on your tombstone?
—What is your strongest conviction? Would you die for it?
—What would you do with a million dollars?

—If the world were to end a year from today, how would you spend your remaining time?

Thoughtful answers to often whimsical questions may trigger any number of essay possibilities. As you toss ideas back and forth in your head, keep your distance from stock responses—those that will lump you with the crowd. Walk around for a few days letting yourself think about what makes you unique. Tell someone what's on your mind. Keep a notebook in your pocket, because a great thought may hit you at any time. Keep pen and pad by your bed to record a four-in-the-morning inspiration. Do some free-writing. Think hard about what you want your readers to think of you. In short, do something to activate your writing muscles.

Some people call this part of the process "prewriting." You might call it getting yourself "psyched." Whatever the name, it's the time you spend messing with possibilities and tuning up to write. It may even include finding a quiet, uncluttered place to work without distractions. It involves laying aside many hours of time for solitary, unhurried work.

> Prewriting may include finding a quiet place for hours of solitary, unhurried work.

Warm-up time should also include a search for the point, or focus, of your essay. Identifying a subject isn't enough. Now you must focus on what you'll say about the subject. The sharper your focus, the better. You can't expect to include everything in a 300- to 500-word essay.

Maybe the surest way to narrow your subject is to begin writing. If your essay seems dull and disappointing after a couple of paragraphs, you're probably being too vague, too impersonal, or both. Keep going, for you may discover the point of your essay at any time. Be prepared, however, to recognize that you may occasionally write yourself into a dead end. Not every subject works. If you find yourself blocked on all sides, you have no choice but to grit your teeth, turn to another topic, and start over.

If you end up dry, even after several attempts, you might try this twenty-question technique for unlocking ideas. Write your subject at the top of a page. Then ask twenty questions about the subject, leaving plenty of space for writing answers. Linda W, for example, knew she wanted to write an essay on dancing, but she didn't know what to say about it. At first she wrote, "During the last eight years dancing has provided me with great satisfaction." Because every devoted ballerina feels exactly the same way, however, Linda realized that the idea was basically boring. So Linda started asking and answering questions like these:

What kind of dancing do I like the most?

When did I first fall in love with dancing?

Why doesn't everybody dance?

What would my life be like without dancing?

Who has been important to me in my dancing? Why?

If I could not dance, what art form would I use to express myself?

What am I giving up or sacrificing by devoting so much time to dance?

How good a dancer am I? How can I find out?

The first questions were easy. When the questions grew hard, both to ask and to answer, Linda had begun to dig deeply into her topic. In figuring out answers, she finally discovered an original point to make in her essay:

> To me, dancing is the most dynamic and personal of the arts. Pictures and sculptures are displayed in museums. Poems and stories are hidden in books. To make music you play someone else's notes on an instrument made by another person. But dancing, ah, dancing, is like life itself.

Where Linda crossed over from prewriting to actually composing her first draft is hard to say, nor is it really necessary. What counts is that she found a topic, narrowed its focus and made a point.

Writing the Essay

By the time some writers begin to compose their essays they more or less know that they'll reach their destination using the famous five-paragraph essay formula. Other writers will start more tentatively, knowing their general direction but not finding the specific route until they get there.

Neither method is better than the other, for much depends on the subject matter and intent of the writer. The first method follows a simple, clear-cut formula, which may not win a prize for originality but can help to turn a muddle of ideas into a model of clarity. It has a beginning, a middle, and an end.

The *formula* is simply an all-purpose plan for arranging ideas into a clear, easy-to-follow order. You have probably used it in school for answering a test question, analyzing a poem or reporting lab work. You can call on it anytime you need to set ideas in order. Its greatest virtue is clarity. Each part has its place and purpose.

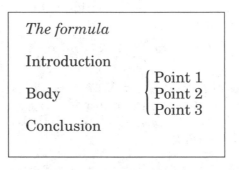

In reality, however, writers rarely follow the *formula*. In fact, you may never see a formula essay in print. Yet a majority of college essays, even those that take circuitous paths between the beginning and end, adhere to some sort of three-step organization. In the *introduction,* writers tell readers what they plan to tell. In the *body* they tell. In the *conclusion* they tell what they told. Since all writers differ, however, you find endless variations within each step, as you're about to see.

Introductions: Hooking the Reader

Use the introduction to let readers know what they're in for. Don't, however, make a formal announcement of your plan: "This essay is about poverty in Manhattan." Just state your point. The reader will recognize the topic soon enough, even without a separate statement of your intention. Maria G, for example, began her essay this way: "Working one weekend a month in Mother Theresa's Soup Kitchen on the lower East Side with the St. Augustine Teen Club has changed my life." This opening promises the reader an account of Maria's weekends in the slums and what the experience has meant to her. It also sets the essay's boundaries. Maria can't include everything about dismal conditions in lower Manhattan. Instead, she'll concentrate on her own experience there, and no more.

The best essays usually begin with something catchy, something to lure the reader into the piece. Basically, it's a hook—a phrase, sentence, or idea that will nab readers' interest so completely that they'll keep on reading almost in spite of themselves. Once you've hooked your readers, you can lead them anywhere.

> The best essays begin with a "hook" to catch the reader's interest.

Hooks must be very sharp, very clean. They must surprise, inform, or tickle the reader in an instant. A dull hook just won't do. Here are a few samples of each:

DULL HOOK

My difficulty in dealing with my feelings probably all started when my parents' marriage started breaking up.

SHARPER HOOK

The first thing I remember is my parents arguing in the next room while I was trying to sleep.

The sharper hook is vivid. It creates a compelling image of a child in the dark, attempting to block out the sounds of his parents' shouting. It also provokes curiosity. The reader wants to know more.

DULL HOOK

The book, *Divine Comedy,* is a serious work of literature, written by Dante several centuries ago.

SHARPER HOOK

Dante's *Divine Comedy,* despite its title, is not a funny book.

The second hook contains a small surprise for the reader. No one who knows Dante's work about the author's travels through Hell, would think of it as humorous. Yet, a student coming to the title for the first time might expect to be amused. The mistake is worth a chuckle—but only if you're familiar with the book.

DULL HOOK

Among my various extracurricular commitments, music has been the most enduring.

SHARPER HOOK

I have tried to immerse myself in music.

In the sharper hook, the terse declaration of the writer's commitment to music makes the point quickly. As the reader, you know instantly that music is the topic. Moreover, the repetition of the "m" sound has a certain appeal.

Naturally, your essay's opening ought to be appropriate to your topic and tone. A serious discussion of Mother Theresa's Soup Kitchen probably shouldn't begin with an irreverent story about a nun. Beware also of any introduction that's too cute or precious. Be thoughtful and clever, yes; obnoxious, no. If you quickly want to lure your reader into your essay, consider any of these five common methods:

> Your opening should be appropriate to your topic and tone.

1. Start with an incident, real or invented, that leads the reader gracefully to the point of your essay.

> "How about 'John Henry' in A?"
> The banjo player kicks off the tune with a solid lead and is joined by the other field pickers in a couple of seconds. Having sung the first verse and chorus, I strum along on the guitar and let my mind wander. How incongruous for me, a product of upper-middle-class suburbia, to be standing in the middle of a grassy field picking bluegrass and old-timey music until dawn.
>
> —Steve M

2. State a provocative idea in an ordinary way or an ordinary idea in a provocative way. Either will spark the reader's interest.

> If you've never been six feet seven inches tall like me, you probably don't know what it's like up here. Everybody is a comedian when they meet you. They call you "Beanpole," or ask, "How's the weather up there?" or tell you to "Watch out for low-flying planes!" Not only that, they expect you to play

basketball, have bumps on your head from doorways, and know things that shorties don't.

—Andy S

3. Use a quotation—not necessarily a famous one. Shakespeare's or your grandmother's will do, as long as it relates to the topic of your essay.

True ease in writing comes from art, not chance,
as those move easiest who have learn'd to dance.
—Alexander Pope,
An Essay on Criticism

It took me eight years to understand Pope's message. I know now that he should have said, "True ease in dance comes from wonderful, frustrating, exciting, tedious, time-consuming, strenuous, and sweaty work, not chance." That may not sound as good, but it's as true.

—Lisa B

4. Knock down a commonly held assumption or define a word in a new and surprising way.

No doubt you've heard that Latin is a dead language. Wrong! Latin is alive and well and living inside my head, thanks to a wonderful teacher who emphasized the culture, not the conjugations, in the language.

—Alicia G

5. Ask an interesting question or two, which you will answer in your essay.

"Tell me, in God's name, why you, Terry D, want to become an English teacher!"

"Because . . . because I want to teach," I stammered. I bent my head, hoping my answers would satisfy him and defuse the unbearable tension that stalked about me.

"Come, Terry, that's not the reason; there's more to it than what you've said. Now why do you want to teach? Is it the kids? The classroom? Power? What force within yourself causes you to associate English and teaching?"

—Teresa D

In any collection of good essays you'd no doubt find other equally worthy techniques for writing a compelling opening. Even a direct statement that introduces your topic may be appropriate. Whatever your opening, it must fit your writing style and personality. Work hard at getting it right, but at the same time, not too hard. An opening that seems forced may irk your reader, and one that comprises, say, more than a quarter of your essay is probably too long.

If you can't find a suitable opening when you begin to write your essay, don't put off writing the rest. As you write the body of the essay, a pleasing idea may hit you. Some writers begin by writing three paragraphs, fully expecting to throw away the first two. They need at least two paragraphs to hit their stride and to rid their minds of extraneous ideas. By the time they've reached paragraph three, they've figured out the point of their essays. Only then do they turn to writing a hook. You might try a similar technique. If your "throwaway" paragraphs contain ideas you can't do without, make room for them later in your essay.

The Body: Putting the Pieces Together

To build a house you must start on the ground. On your foundation you construct a frame, then add walls, a roof, a TV antenna—and you're done! The builder must follow this order or the house will crumble.

Order is important to the writer, too. What should come first? Second? Third? In most writing the best order is the clearest order, the arrangement your reader can follow with the least effort.

Just as a highway map shows several routes from one town to another, there is no single way to get from the beginning of a piece of writing to the end. The route you take depends on the purpose of the trip. The order of ideas in the body of your essay will vary according to what you want to do to your reader. Whether you want to shock, sadden, inspire, inform, or entertain the reader, each purpose will have its own best order. In storytelling, the events are often placed in the sequence in which they occur. To explain a childhood memory or define who you are, to stand up for gay rights or describe a poignant moment—each may take some other particular arrangement. No one plan is superior to another, provided you have a valid reason for using it.

The plan that fails is the aimless one, the one in which ideas are arranged solely on the basis of the order in which they popped into your head. To guard against aimlessness, rank your ideas in order of importance either before you start or while you're writing drafts. Although your first idea may turn out to be your best, you probably should save it for later in your essay. Giving it away at the start is self-defeating. To hold your reader's interest, it's better to work toward your best point, not away from it. If you have, say, three main points to make, save the strongest for last. Launch your essay with your second best, and tuck your least favorite between the other two.

> To hold the reader's interest, work toward your best point, not away from it.

In a typical college essay, a body consisting of three sections will be just about right. Why *three*? Mainly because three is a number that works. When you can make three statements about a subject, you probably know what you're talking about. One is too simple, and two is still pretty shallow, but three is thoughtful. Psychologically, three creates a sense of wholeness, like the beginning, middle, and end of a story. Each point doesn't necessarily receive equal treatment. You might manage one point with a single paragraph, but the others may get more. Each point has to be distinctive: Your third point mustn't be a rerun of the first or second.

It shouldn't be difficult to break the main point of most essays into at least three secondary points, regardless of their topic or form. A narrative essay, for example, naturally breaks into a beginning, middle, and end. A process is likely to have at least three steps, some of which may be broken into substeps. In an essay of comparison and contrast, you ought to be able to find at least three similarities and differences to write about. A similar division into thirds applies to essays of cause and effect, definition and description, and certainly to essays of argumentation.

Turn back to the sample essays in Chapter 2. Each of the successful pieces follows the three-part pattern. In rough outline, they look like this:

Chandra's essay (page 35)

Subject:	The struggles within me
Point 1:	What do I stand for?
Point 2:	What should I do with my life?
Point 3:	How can I communicate with others?

Angela's essay (page 37)

Subject:	My field hockey career
Point 1:	Starting out in ninth grade—a social activity
Point 2:	In tenth and eleventh grade—fun and dedication
Point 3:	Becoming a champion—a serious commitment

Eric's essay (page 39)

Subject:	Joint custody
Point 1:	Description of my weekly ordeal
Point 2:	My relationship with my mother and father
Point 3:	How joint custody has changed me

Only Joyce's essay (page 33) defies analysis into three sections. In fact, the piece fails for the very reason that Joyce tried to make more than half a dozen points. Each point remains undeveloped, and in the end the essay is little more than a list of Joyce's interests and activities.

Transitions and Paragraphs: Taking Readers by the Hand

Readers need to be led. As you write, think of readers as tourists and your essay as a trip they take from one place to another. You are their guide, their travel agent.

After you've told them where they're going (the introduction), keep reminding them (in the body of the essay) where they're headed. In long essays readers need more reminders than in short ones. To keep readers well informed, you don't have to repeat what you've written, but rather plant key ideas, slightly rephrased, as milestones along the way. (The sentence you just read contains just such a marker. The phrase *"To keep a reader well informed"* prompts you to keep in mind the topic being discussed—that is, helping readers find their way.) Watch out for detours, for you may lose your readers if you step too far outside the path you laid out at the start. (The sentence you just read is a detour. Yes, it's related to the topic but it steers the discussion away from guiding readers through an essay.)

Help readers along, too, by choosing words that set up relation-ships between one idea and the next. This can be done with such words as *this,* which ties the sentence you are now reading, for example, to the previous one. The English language supplies many words and phrases for tying sentences and ideas together, among them:

also	on the other hand	still
too	consequently	another
further	therefore	finally
in addition	although	in the first place
similarly	moreover	regardless
as a result	nevertheless	on the contrary
however	now	better still
for instance	this	yet

Each time you link one sentence to another with a transitional word or phrase, you help to clear a path for readers through your writing. Without such help, or when every sentence stands uncon-nected to the next, readers may end up hopelessly lost, like travel-ers going down roads without signposts or markers.

Links between sentences lend a hand to writers, too. They help them stick to the topic. Ideas that don't connect with others around them probably should be moved or thrown out.

The inventor of the paragraph also figured out a simple way to mark the path through a piece of writing. The paragraph indenta-tion is a signal to readers to get ready for a change in thought or idea, somewhat like the directional blinker telling other drivers that you're about to turn.

Yet, not every new paragraph signals a drastic change. The writer may simply want to move the essay ahead one step at a time, and paragraphs illuminate each step.

Some paragraphs spring directly from those that came before. Like infants, they can't stand alone. The paragraph before this one, for example, is linked to the previous one by the connecting word *yet.* The connection has cued you to get ready for a contrast-ing thought, but it also reminded you that the two paragraphs are related.

Abrupt starts are best from time to time. Suddenness will sur-prise and keep readers alert. Connecting words will dilute the impact of the surprise. Be wary of a string of abrupt starts, however, because too many quick shifts may annoy more than surprise.

Paragraphs let your readers skip rapidly through your work, particularly when each first or last sentence summarizes the rest of the paragraph. Readers may then focus on paragraph openings and closings and skip what's in between. Readers in a hurry will appreciate that, but you can force readers to linger a while by varying the location of the most important idea in each paragraph.

Whether your readers skim the paragraphs or slog doggedly through every word, they need to find sentences now and then that, like landmarks, help them to know where they are. Such guiding sentences differ from others because they define the paragraph's main topic; hence the name *topic sentence.*

Most, but not all, paragraphs contain topic sentences. The topic of some paragraphs is so obvious that to state it would be redundant. Then, too, groups of paragraphs can be so closely knit that one topic sentence states the most important idea for all of them.

No rule governs every possible use of a topic sentence. A sense of what readers need in order to understand your meaning must guide you. Consider your readers absent-minded wanderers. Since they tend to lose their way, remind them often about where they are. Let the topic sentences lead. If in doubt, grasp their hands too firmly rather than too loosely. Follow the principle that if there is any way to misunderstand or misinterpret your words, readers will most certainly find it.

> Consider your readers absent-minded wanderers. Remind them often where they are.

The Conclusion: Giving a Farewell Gift

When you reach the end of your essay, you can lift your pen off the page and be done with it. Better still, you can present your reader with a little something to remember you by, a *gift*—an idea to think about, a line to chuckle over, a memorable phrase or quotation. Whatever you give, the farewell gift must fit the content, style, and mood of your essay. A tacked-on ending will puzzle, not delight, your readers.

> Send your readers off feeling glad that they stayed with you to the end.

Some writers think that endings are more important than beginnings. After all, by the time readers arrive at the conclusion, the introduction may have already begun to fade from memory. A stylish ending, though, will stick with them and influence their feelings about your essay and, of course, about its writer. Therefore, choose a farewell gift thoughtfully. Be particular. Send your readers off feeling good or laughing, weeping, angry, thoughtful, or thankful, but above all, glad that they stayed with your essay to the end.

A conclusion that's too pat or common will leave readers with the impression that you were too cheap to give the best gift you could, or that you chose your gift in haste. Stay away especially from bargain-basement gifts like these:

> The challenges I faced will help me in college and in the future. (from an essay on a significant experience)

> Then I woke up and saw that it was all a dream. (from an essay about talking with a famous person in history)

> I'd recommend this book to anyone who likes good psychological or murder stories. (from an essay about *Crime and Punishment,* an influential book in the writer's life)

> In conclusion, if I can be half as successful as my aunt, I will have fulfilled myself as an individual. (from an influential person essay)

Such trite endings suggest that the writers couldn't think of anything original to say or that they just wanted to get their essays over with. Either way, a stale conclusion can spoil a good essay.

Readers will appreciate almost any gift you give them, provided you've put some thought into your choice. When writing the ending, let your instinct guide you. You've read enough stories and plays and have heard enough songs to know what endings sound like, what lends a sense of completeness to a creative piece of work. For example, when you tell readers how an unresolved issue was settled, or when you speculate on what might occur in the future, readers sense that an ending is at hand.

Even commonly used endings can be turned into stylish gifts, as these samples show:

1. Have some fun with your ending. A reader may remember your sense of humor long after forgetting other details about you.

SUBJECT

Elizabeth H, an active member of many groups, treasures the hours she has for herself.

GIFT
___

Thoreau's remark, "I love to be alone," might well be my senior quote. In spite of the incessant plea of the telephone company to "reach out and touch someone," there are some of us who would prefer to remain untouched. I am one of them.

SUBJECT
___

Debbie B's lifelong competition with her sister Michelle ended when Michelle left for college.

GIFT
___

. . . I stepped right into my sister's shoes (figuratively, not literally—because Michelle has a size five compared to my seven and a half). I think that my brain would become seriously warped if my feet were that squished.

2. End with an apt quotation, drawn either from the essay itself or from elsewhere.

SUBJECT
___

Craig S had to find safe shelter during a wilderness adventure.

GIFT
___

At that point I knew by instinct, "This is the place."

SUBJECT
___

Frank F had a part-time job in a hotel kitchen when a terrible fire broke out.

GIFT
___

To this day, whenever I smell food garbage, I hear the words, "Fire! Fire! Fire!" and the clang of fire bells.

3. Finish with a clear restatement of your essay's main point, using new words. Add a short tag line, perhaps.

SUBJECT

Carol B tells how she changed between ninth and eleventh grades.

GIFT

The main difference in me is that now I like myself. I could be friends with someone like me.

SUBJECT

Ian B learned about himself while reading Moss Hart's autobiography, *Act One.*

GIFT

There are no limits to the human spirit, no obstacles large enough to impede the attainment of a dream, provided that one's resolve and determination are equal to all the discouraging effects of failure. Further, there is no sin in initial failure. That's what I keep telling myself.

4. Bring the reader up to date or project him into the future.

SUBJECT

Ellen G tells of an old woman she met while working as a volunteer in a nursing home.

GIFT

I still visit Mrs. Thurnauer. Some weeks she is more vibrant than others. Even on her bad days I see her intelligence and courage. And even if on a certain day her hair is not combed back as smoothly as when I first met her, she still reminds me that growing old is not always a desperate process, in which all pride and hope are lost.

SUBJECT

Jonathan M hopes to become a well-known (and rich) artist.

GIFT

Someday, collectors and museums may want to hang my paintings on their walls. I am always hopeful. Nevertheless, I am playing the lottery this week. The jackpot is $20 million and the odds of winning are only one in three million. I hope the probability is more favorable in the art world.

Above all, avoid the summary ending. Trust your reader to remember the substance of your one- or two-page essay. To say everything again is not only pointless, it borders on being an insult to the reader's intelligence. Your essay isn't a textbook. A chapter review isn't necessary.

Some essays don't need an extended conclusion. When they're over, they're over. Even a short conclusion is better than none at all, however. At the end, readers should feel that they've arrived somewhere. In a sense, every well-planned essay prepares readers for arrival at a certain destination. The introduction tells readers approximately where they're going. En route, a series of ideas propels them toward the conclusion. At the end they're welcomed with a thoughtful gift. When they get to the last word, you don't want readers to say, "Oh, now I see what you've been driving at."

5 REWRITING AND EDITING

This could be the hardest part of writing an essay. You've invested a lot of yourself in the work by this time. You won't want to go back now and start changing things. Who can blame you? Try, however, to resist the impulse to rest. It's not time, yet.

Perhaps you're willing to alter a word here and there, check the spelling, relocate a comma or two, and repair a bit of broken-down grammar, but that's proofreading, not rewriting—and it's definitely not enough right now. Proofreading requires skills, but rewriting takes courage. It's painful work, for you may end up discarding large chunks of your essay and rewriting parts you've already rewritten. After you've struggled to get a paragraph just right, it's hard to give it up. Be brave. The next one you write may be even better.

> Being tough on yourself is a courtesy to your readers.

Having Another Look

The root of revision is the word *vision,* that is, sight or perception. When revising, you *look again* to see whether you have said what you intended, and arranged your ideas in the best possible order. If you perceive a flaw or weakness, then revise—that is, *rewrite.* Read your essay ten, maybe twenty, times. During each reading, inspect it with a different set of lenses. Read it often for overall impression, but also to check it for each of these qualities:

—*Accuracy.* Have you answered the question on the application?

—*Purpose.* What do you want the reader to think of you after reading the essay? Have you portrayed yourself accurately? Does the essay sound like you?

—*Focus.* Have you limited the subject enough to cover it well in a fairly short essay?

—*Main idea.* What is the message you want to leave in the reader's mind?

—*Unity.* Do you stick to the point from beginning to end? Do you keep reminding the reader of the point? Have you tied ideas together?

—*Organization.* Does your introduction draw readers into the essay? Can you explain the order of ideas in the body of your essay? What does your ending add to the essay?

—*Development.* What is the main point of each paragraph? What does each paragraph contribute to the whole? Have you said enough in each paragraph?

Being tough on yourself is a courtesy to your readers. College admissions officials have plenty to do. You'll spare them extra work by doing all you can to make your writing clear. Readers crave clarity. They want to understand what you say. They won't do your thinking for you, however. Don't assume, "They'll know what I mean." Tell them *exactly* what you mean. By doing so, you'll improve not only the essay but also your chances of getting in.

As you rewrite, deprive the readers of every possible chance to stretch, garble, or misconstrue your meaning. Here are some methods you might try:

—*Read your essay aloud. Your ear is a good instrument for detecting words that don't sound right.*

—*Let someone read your essay aloud to you. Listen carefully, and watch his or her face for telltale signs of confusion or doubt.*

—*Let your essay cool for a while—a few hours, a day or so. When you come back, try to read it with the eyes of a stranger.*

The more rewriting you do, the better your essay is likely to be. On the other hand, you could write yourself right out of the essay. Too much painstaking revision may deprive the essay of its personality. The trick is to rewrite repeatedly but to make the words sound natural and spontaneous. Writers work for a long time to perfect the technique.

Finding Your "Voice"

In almost every essay that you're likely to write for a college, a natural, conversational style is appropriate. Since the essay should be personal, the language should sound like you. When you use the pretentious language of a senator, the formal words of a legal document, or the slick style of, say, a TV commercial, you're going to sound like a senator, a lawyer, or a copywriter, not like yourself.

Don't imitate anyone. Just let your genuine voice ring out. If you think of your writing voice as the sound of your words in a diary or letter to a friend, you'll be getting close. Don't confuse "voice" with speech, however. Voice conveys the personality behind the words. It's not necessary to cram your essay with street talk, half-formed sentences, or pop expressions in order to sound real. Rather, consider the voice in your essay as natural speech, shorn of trendy words and expressions, and also grammatically correct, perhaps the casual speech of someone who speaks exceedingly well. As a rule, you might steer clear of writing anything that you'd feel uncomfortable saying aloud in a class discussion or in a friendly conversation with the head of your school.

> Don't imitate. Just let your genuine voice ring out.

Question: Can you find Becky's voice in this passage?

> I desire so fervently to attend Amherst because I believe it is the only school that will enable me to explore my intellectual capabilities, heighten my perception of knowledge and gain a greater insight into myself and a greater understanding of others, in an atmosphere of united support for the individual.

No doubt, Becky wants Amherst, but she sounds more like a candidate for public office than a candidate for college. She conceals herself behind high-blown language that may sound important and profound but says very little—very little that's *clear*, at any rate. Contrast this with a passage from Lisa's essay about why she chose Wesleyan:

> During my visit in October, I had a good feeling about the academic life on the campus. It offers so much. I didn't want to go home and back to high school. Everyone I talked to in the dorm seemed happy about being in college there. If I am accepted, I'm sure that I will be bitten by the same bug of enthusiasm.

The voice you hear in Lisa's essay belongs to a genuine person. As she talks, you could be sitting next to her on the bus. Although informal, the writing is controlled.

You hear another kind of voice in this excerpt from the opening of Alec's essay for Columbia:

> You ask me to write an essay about myself. Eh? What can I say? Could Napoleon have written an essay about himself? Oh, what the hell, why not give it a crack, eh what?
> When I indulge in one of my favorite activities, thinking about myself, the word *unique* kicks around the old noggin. . . .

Alec sounds like a smart aleck. You'd never guess that he's a deep and discerning thinker. Later in the piece, however, he stops babbling and finds a more honest voice. Breezy it is, but no longer obnoxious:

> Enough about my intellectual musings (and what amusing musings they are). Another field of interest I cultivated in lieu of physical activity was acting. In the eight years that I have acted professionally, having appeared off Broadway and on a CBS movie of the week, I have basically developed into a character actor. However, I have been working on playing more natural parts lately, and even though I still play character parts, they have become less caricatured and more natural.
> Although I intend to pursue acting as a career, I don't intend to major in it. For two reasons: (1) I have other scholarly interests, and (2) I'm a klutz and could never wait on tables to support myself, so I hope to teach instead.

You can check your writing voice by having a friend hand your essay to someone who doesn't know you. If a stranger can describe you accurately after reading your work, you can safely say that you've been faithful to yourself.

Editing for Clarity

You probably started editing your essay soon after composing the first few lines. That is, you changed and reworded sentences to make certain they said what you wanted them to say. As you continue, regard every word and phrase as a potential threat to the clarity of your writing. Ask yourself repeatedly: Is this the clearest word for me to use here? Are these words arranged in the clearest order?

Plain Words

To write clearly, use plain words. Never use a complex word because it sounds good or it makes you seem more mature. A college essay is not the place to show off your vocabulary. Use a so-called SAT word only when necessary—that is, when it's the only word that will add something to the essay's tone and meaning, which you'll lose by using a common word. Keep that thesaurus on the shelf unless you are stuck. An elegant word used merely to use an elegant word is bombastic . . . er . . . big sounding and unnatural.

> A college essay is not the place to show off your vocabulary.

Simple ideas dressed up in ornate words often obscure meaning. Worse, they make the writer sound phony, if not foolish. For example, you wouldn't say, "I'm going to my *domicile*" after a day at school, and you don't call your teachers *pedagogues*. Yet, this overblown sentence appeared on the draft of an essay for Northwestern; "My history pedagogue insisted that I labor in my domicile for two hours each night." How much clearer to have written, "My history teacher assigned two hours' homework every night."

Notice how clear these sentences sound when the inflated words are removed:

FANCY

The more I recalled her degradation of me, the more inexorable I became.

PLAIN

The more I thought of her insults, the more determined I grew.

FANCY

During that year, my proclivities toward Italian art were instigated.

PLAIN

During that year, I began to favor Italian art.

FANCY

I learned the importance of cordiality and cooperation in a competitive racing situation.

PLAIN

I learned that teamwork pays off in a race.

Please don't interpret this plea for plain words as an endorsement of everyday slang. If you need an expression like *airhead, chill,* and *pig out,* or a comic book word like *gonna* and *gotta,* by all means use it. For heaven's sake, though, use such words sparingly and only to create an effect you can't do without. Don't highlight a word with "quotes" to signal that you know it's nonstandard. If to make its point your essay overdoses on slang, be sure to show your mastery of standard English by writing another part of your application in good, straightforward prose.

English is loaded with simple words that can express the most profound ideas. Descartes' famous observation, "I think. Therefore, I am," reshaped forever the way we think about existence. Descartes may have used esoteric language to make his point, but the very simplicity of his words endows his statement with great power. Ernest Hemingway called a writer's greatest gift "a built-in, shock-proof crap detector." Hemingway's own detector worked well. He produced about the leanest, plainest writing in the English language—not that you should try to emulate Hemingway, although you could do worse, but an efficient crap detector will encourage you to choose words only because they say exactly what you mean.

Exact Words

It's often hard to break away from using vague, shadowy, and abstract words. If you want your ideas to sink into the minds of readers, however, give them exact, clear, and well-defined words. Almost always, exact words help you express exact thoughts. Since a tight, precise, hard-edged word has an unmistakable meaning, give the reader a *wooden bucket* instead of a *container,* a *blazing sunset* instead of a *beautiful evening, white-haired and stooped* instead of *old,* and a *Big Mac, large fries, and coke* instead of *lunch.*

To write with exact words is to write with pictures, sounds, and actions that are as vivid in words as in reality. Exact words hit harder than hazy ones:

HAZY

Quite violently, I expressed my anger to the other team's player.

EXACT

I punched the Bruins' goalie in the nose and sent him sprawling.

HAZY

Skiing is a sport I enjoy, not only for the esthetics, but also for the art and skill involved.

EXACT

I like to ski, not just to see snow-decked pines and brilliant sky, but also to weave gracefully down steep slopes.

Of course, you need abstract words, too. Words such as *beauty, love, existence, nobility,* and *envy* stand for ideas that exist in the mind. The power to think in terms of *situations, concepts, feelings,* and *principles* is unique to humans. An essay full of vague, hard-to-define words and ideas, though, will leave your reader at sea about what you are trying to say. A student who writes about an "ugly" teacher, for example, sends a different image of an ugly person to each reader. If the teacher is *a ragged, slouching beast,* the writer should say so. Or if the teacher's personality is ugly, the student should write *ill-tempered and aloof* or show the teacher shouting harsh threats at the hapless class.

Anticipate reactions to every word. Ask yourself, "Might readers understand this word in any other way than how I meant it?" If so, strike it out and find another.

Although exact words will always be clearer than abstract ones, a word or phrase with multiple meanings may often help to tighten your writing. Every time you mention *dinner,* for example, you need not list the menu. Be aware, though, that nobody will care to read an essay that forgot to come down to earth.

Clear Sentences

Short sentences are the clearest—sometimes. Use a short sentence to emphasize a point. Sometimes you may need long sentences to convey complex ideas, although a complex thought may just as easily be expressed in clear, short sentences. When trapped in a long, strung-out sentence, break it into a set of shorter sentences. Later, if necessary, you can put the pieces together again.

Now and then you may run into a long-winded sentence that suffers from paralysis. No matter how you tinker with it you can't make it move without damaging its meaning. Walk away from it and repair it later, or try a few manipulations. Here, to illustrate a stubborn case, is a rambling bit of prose that needs fixing:

> A sentence can be molded into almost any shape, beautiful or ugly.

> One of my biggest rewards has been the computer club, which was formed in my junior year, at which time the club members were informed by the computer teacher of a computer contest that was being conducted by Fairfield University.

REMEDY	RESULTS (Some Better Than Others)
Break the long sentence into shorter ones.	One of my biggest rewards has been the computer club, which was formed in my junior year. At that time Fairfield University was conducting a computer contest. The computer teacher informed the club members about it.
	or
	One of my biggest rewards has been the computer club. It was formed in my junior year. When the club started, the computer teacher informed the members about a computer contest at Fairfield University.
Move words from predicate to subject.	A computer club has been one of my biggest rewards . . .
	A computer club, formed in my junior year, has been one of my biggest rewards.
	or
Combine ideas; turn less important ideas into phrases.	Formed in my junior year, a computer club . . .
Change nouns to adjectives.	My most rewarding activity has been a computer club . . .
Change nouns to verbs.	Computer club activities have rewarded me . . .

Change verbs to nouns.	The formation of a computer club . . .
Switch the focus.	A contest at Fairfield University introduced me to the rewards of working with computers . . .

or

My computer teacher introduced me to the most rewarding work . . .

or

I got my start with computers after my teacher . . .

Once you start such sentence manipulations, you may begin to see endless possibilities. A sentence is much like clay. It's malleable and can be molded into almost any shape, beautiful or ugly. In the end the sentence should stand in the form that expresses most clearly and accurately what you want to say.

Clear Meaning

In your writing, words must fit together like the pieces of a jigsaw puzzle. Sometimes a word looks as though it fits, but it doesn't. A misplaced word may produce a rather peculiar sentence. Take these, for example:

> While running to English class, the bell rang.
> Working full-time, the summer went by quickly.
> When only eight years old, my father warned me about smoking.

These may not strike you as funny at first. Look again. Do you see that these sentences describe a weird world in which bells run to class, summers hold full-time jobs, and youthful fathers dispense advice?

The authors of these sentences have tried to join two pieces that don't fit. The grammar is flawless; the spelling and punctuation are perfect. Even the writers' intentions are clear. In each sentence, however, the parts are mismatched. After the comma in each, readers expect to find out who is running, who was working, and who is just eight years old. They don't. They're left dangling. (Hence, the name *dangling modifier* or *dangling participle* has been assigned to this type of sentence construction.)

To keep the reader from dangling, the writers might have said:

> While the boys were running to English class, the bell rang.
> Since Charlotte worked full-time, her summer sped by.
> When I was eight, my father warned me about smoking.

Relative pronouns (*who, whose, whom, that,* and *which*) may also lead to problems of clarity. Perhaps such words may not deserve a reputation as troublemakers, but like a black sheep in the family, they have it just the same. They've acquired their name—*relative* pronoun—from their intimate relationship with another word in the same sentence, called an *antecedent.*

A relative pronoun and an antecedent are related because one refers directly to the other. In this sentence,

> It's always my brother who is blamed for trouble in the neighborhood.

the relative pronoun "*who*" and the antecedent "*brother*" are right next to each other, about as close as kin can be. In this sentence,

> It's always my brother, now approaching his twentieth birthday, who is blamed for trouble in the neighborhood.

the phrase "*now approaching his twentieth birthday*" intrudes, thereby weakening the relationship, but the meaning is still clear.

You run into a particular problem with pronouns when you try to establish a tie between the pronoun *which,* for example, and a whole series of actions, feelings or words, as in

> First we had lunch and then our guide told us the secret of the cave, which pleased me.

A reader might honestly wonder what was "pleasing." The cave's secret? The guide's spilling the beans? Lunch? That the secret was revealed after lunch? The pronoun "*which*" might refer to all or to only one of these possible antecedents. It's just not clear. To repair the sentence you might change it into something like this:

> I was pleased that the guide waited until after lunch to tell us the secret of the cave.

If another meaning was intended,

> I was pleased with the secret of the cave, which the guide
> told us after lunch.

Another sort of pronoun, namely the word *this,* creates similar problems of clarity. Any time you start a sentence with *this,* double-check it. Make sure it refers directly to what you want it to refer. This is advice you should not ignore!

Harmony

Writers, like music makers, strive for harmony in their art. Every chamber ensemble, barbershop quartet, and reggae, rap, or rock group works hard to achieve a pleasing and unified sound, and you can tell almost instantly whether they've done it. Likewise, when you write an essay, you have to work on blending the parts harmoniously. A discordant essay—one in which the pieces seem disconnected—will leave your readers confused.

As you edit your application essay, read it over repeatedly for its internal harmony. That is, check to see if one idea seems to lead naturally and easily to the next. Look for words and phrases that tie ideas together. (Turn to page 76 for some common examples of transitions.) In a harmonious essay, virtually every sentence bears some sort of reference to the sentence that came before. Such references might be obvious, as in "furthermore" or "for example." They are often more subtle, however, as in this pair of sentences:

> I have an idealized image in my mind of families that are
> close, loving, laughing, generous, and supportive.
> I wish that I could find *such qualities* in mine.

Notice that the italicized phrase in the second sentence refers directly to adjectives listed in the first.

Sometimes, however, allusions to previous sentences are carried in the meaning rather than by a specific word or phrase:

> I had a hard time finding his house in the dark.
> I *picked out what I thought should be the address* and
> knocked at the front door.

In this example the italicized words establish a link to the idea stated in the first sentence. In the second sentence the speaker feels unsure of an address. You know the reason (because it's dark outside) only because you know what the first sentence says.

Search your essay for transitions of all kinds. Whenever you discover a series of three or more sentences devoid of transitions, you may be stuck with a hard-to-read muddle on your hands. Before you do any heavy rewriting, though, try inserting appropriate transitional words, phrases, and sentences. Don't wedge one in where it doesn't belong, however. This could confuse your readers even more.

As you've no doubt realized, editing a piece of writing is a meticulous process. When you examine every word you write, it's easy to drown in a sea of minutiae. Therefore, it helps now and then to stop fussing over the details and to inspect your essay as a whole. Say aloud to yourself or to anyone within earshot, "The point of my essay is . . ." Complete the statement with one clear, straightforward declarative sentence. If it takes more than a single statement, perhaps your essay isn't sufficiently focused. You may be trying to say more than you have space for.

> Now and then, stop fussing over details, and inspect your essay as a whole.

After you've declared your main point, try to say what each part adds to the whole. If any part does not seem to contribute, cast it away. You don't need material that sends readers off the course you've set for them. By attending to the contents of the whole essay, you are in a sense checking its harmony, determining whether all its parts work together in unison.

An outline of your essay will help, too. Such an outline need not follow the formal pattern you may have learned in school, but the same principle applies. That is, all the minor pieces, when added together, should equal the whole. In the language of writers, every sentence in a paragraph supports the main idea of the paragraph, and every paragraph supports the main idea of the essay. You'll know that you have a well-structured, harmonious piece of writing when you can't reasonably remove a piece without causing damage to the whole.

Editing for Interest

Don't bore your readers. Admissions officials may ignore an occasional lapse in clarity and even overlook a flaw in grammar, but if your essay bores them, they'll lose interest in both you and your essay.

Like most applicants, you've probably led a fairly routine life. That's no reason, however, to write a routine essay. Fortunately, there are plenty of techniques for turning an ordinary piece of writing into a highly readable and stylish essay.

Brevity Works Best

Never use two words when one will do. Readers want to be told quickly and directly what you have to say. Wordiness sucks the life out of your writing. Cut out needless words. Readers value economy.

(Stop! Go back to the previous paragraph. Do you see the unnecessary words? Did you notice that the next-to-last sentence reiterates the first? Yes, the statement contains only four words, but are those words necessary? Do they merely add weight—and no substance—to the paragraph?)

Your sentences, like muscles, should be firm and tight. Needless words are flabby. Trim the fat. Make your writing lean. As you edit, exercise your crossing-out muscles.

Go through every sentence and cross out extra words. The sentence you just read contains nine words (forty-three letters). It could be trimmed still more. For example, "Cut extra words out of every sentence" (seven words, thirty-one letters). When the sentence was first written, it read, "The writer should work through all the sentences he writes by examining each one and crossing out all the extra words" (twenty-one words, ninety-seven letters)—three times longer than the trim, seven-word model, and three times duller.

In lean writing every word counts. One missing word distorts or changes the meaning. To trim your sentences, squeeze them through your fat detector:

1. Look for repetition. Then combine sentences.

___

FAT

In tenth grade I accepted a position at Wilkins' Fabrics. In this position I learned about fabrics and about how to handle customers. (23 words)

___

TRIMMED

In tenth grade I accepted a position at Wilkins' Fabrics, where I learned about fabrics and handling customers. (18)

RETRIMMED

Working at Wilkins' Fabrics since tenth grade, I have learned to handle both fabrics and customers. (16)

2. Look for telltale words like *which, who, that, thing,* and *all*. They may indicate the presence of fat.

FAT

Manicotti is a dish *that* I always enjoy eating. (9)

TRIMMED

I like manicotti any time. (5)

FAT

Jogging has been a wonderful activity, *which* has stimulated my body and freed my mind to think. (17)

TRIMMED

Jogging has been wonderful for stimulating my body and freeing my mind. (12)

FAT

The *thing* that made me angry was mosquitoes inside my shirt. (11)

TRIMMED

Mosquitoes inside my shirt angered me. (6)

3. Look for phrases that add words but little meaning.

FAT

At this point in time, I am not able to say. (11)

TRIMMED

I can't say now. (4)

FAT

The chef stayed home *as a result of* his not feeling well. (12)

TRIMMED

The chef stayed home because he felt sick. (8)

A Baker's Dozen Specially Selected Fat Phrases—No, Make That Thirteen Selected Fat Phrases:

FAT	*TRIMMED*
what I mean is	I mean
after all is said and done	finally
for all intents and purposes	(omit)
in the final analysis	finally
few and far between	few
each and every one	each
this is a subject that	this subject
ten in number	ten
at the age of six years old	at age six
most unique	unique
true fact	fact
biography of his life	biography
in regard to, with regard to, in relation to, with reference to	about

Readers are too busy for sentences stuffed with fat phrases.

After your sentences are pared to the bone, look at what remains and get ready to cut some more. Although it hurts to take out what you worked hard to put in, the writing will be stronger, more readable, and noticeably more interesting.

Show, Don't Tell

The genius who invented "show and tell" realized that seeing a pet frog or a souvenir model of Grant's Tomb was far more interesting to an audience than just hearing about it. Since writers can't use hands, make faces, or dangle an object in front of readers, writers must rely on words to do both the telling and the showing.

> Show more than you tell. Use words to make the reader see.

Show more than you tell. Use words to make the reader *see*. For example, don't leave the reader guessing about Laura's beautiful hair. *Show* how the breeze catches the edge of her silky, brown hair. Don't just tell about the garbage in the hallway. *Show* the splintered glass lying in the oily water, the half-torn notebook, and the newspaper, yellowed with age. Don't just say you felt happy. *Show* yourself bounding down the steps four at a time, coat unzipped, shouting into the wind, "Hurray, I did it!"

TELL

After I won, I experienced a wonderful and unique feeling, which makes me want to win again.

SHOW

After I won, my sense of accomplishment grew with every handshake and pat on the back. My face ached from grinning so much. I knew that I'd be back next year to win again.

TELL

There is so much I have to do after school that I often don't even have time for homework.

SHOW

The busy part of my life starts at three o'clock: pick up Scott, my baby brother; piano lessons on Tuesdays at four; French Club; work on the newspaper; and tutor my neighbor in math. I don't have time for homework, not to mention working out.

When words show what you have in mind, the reader can see and feel and hear what you saw and felt and heard. It takes details—lots and lots of them—to make a sight or sound or smell as real for the reader as it is for you.

Your essay would soon grow tedious—both to write and to read—if you showed every grain of sand on the beach. Be selective. Show readers the sights you want them to *see:* the gleaming sand and fragments of clam shells; to *hear:* the squawk of gulls and children's shouts; to *smell:* salt spray, seaweed, and suntan oil; to *feel:* stinging feet and sweaty, sun-baked backs; and to *taste:* gritty egg salad sandwiches and parched, salt-caked lips.

Although too much detail can be boring, too little is just as bad. A balance is best. No one can tell you exactly how to achieve that balance. You need time to get the feel of it. Like walking a tightrope, riding a bike, or doing a back flip, it becomes instinct after a while. The context, as well as your judgment of the reader's intelligence, will have to determine how detailed you need to be. To get the knack a little more quickly, study a written passage that you found interesting. Pick out both details and broad statements. Use the passage as a general model for your own writing, but give it your own stamp. After all, it's your voice the reader wants to hear.

Active Verbs

At some point you must have learned that a verb is a word that shows *action* or *state of being*. That's a fair description of a verb if you're learning grammar. To an essay writer, however, knowing that *action* verbs differ from *being* verbs is far more important. You need active verbs to stimulate interest. Since active verbs describe or show movement, they create life. They perform, stir up, get up, and move around. They excel over all other words in their power to pump vitality into your writing. They add energy and variety to sentences. As a bonus, active verbs often help you trim needless words from your writing.

> Active verbs pump life into your writing.

In contrast, being verbs are stagnant. They don't do anything. Notice the lifelessness in all the most common forms of the verb *to be: is, are, was, were, am, has been, had been, will be*. When used in a sentence, each of these being verbs joins the subject to the predicate—and that's all. In fact, the verb *to be* acts much like an equals sign in an equation, as in "Four minus three is one" ($4 - 3 = 1$), "Harold is smart" (Harold = smart), or "That is some spicy meatball" (That = SSMB). Because equals signs (and being verbs) show no action, use active verbs whenever you can.

Being verbs are perfectly acceptable in speech and writing. In fact, it's hard to get along without them. Be stingy, however. If more than, say, one-fourth of your sentences use a form of *to be* as the main verb, perhaps you're relying too heavily on being verbs.

Substitute active verbs for being verbs by extracting them from other words in the same sentence. For instance:

BEING VERB

Linda was the winner of the raffle.

ACTIVE VERB

Linda won the raffle.
Here the verb *"won"* has been extracted from the noun *"winner."* Active verbs may also be extracted from adjectives, as in:

BEING VERB

My summer at the New Jersey shore was enjoyable.

ACTIVE VERB

I enjoyed my summer at the New Jersey shore.
Sometimes it pays to substitute an altogether fresh verb.

BEING VERB

It is not easy for me to express my feelings.

ACTIVE VERB

I find it difficult to express my feelings.

BEING VERB

There was a distant wailing of an ambulance.

ACTIVE VERB

We heard the distant wailing of an ambulance.

Practice will help you purge being verbs from your sentences and add vitality to whatever you write.

The noun you employ as the subject of a sentence will often determine your chances of using a lively verb. Abstract nouns limit your opportunities. For example, you're almost compelled to use a form of *to be* in any sentence that begins with *"The reason,"* as in *"The reason I am applying to Colgate* is." You have few verb choices, too, when the subject of the sentence is *thought, concept, idea, issue, way, cause,* or any other abstract noun.

On the other hand, nouns that stand for specific people, places, events, and objects take active verbs easily. When your sentence contains a subject that can do something—a person, for instance—you can choose from among thousands of active verbs. Anytime you replace a general or abstract noun with a solid, easy-to-define noun, you are likely to end up with a tight, energetic, and generally more interesting sentence:

ABSTRACT SUBJECT

The issue was settled by Mrs. Marino.

DEFINITE SUBJECT

Mrs. Marino settled the issue.

ABSTRACT SUBJECT

The cause of the strike was the students' demand for peace.

DEFINITE SUBJECT

The students struck for peace.

ABSTRACT SUBJECT

The way to Memorial Hospital is down this road.

DEFINITE SUBJECT

This road goes to Memorial Hospital.

Being verbs aren't alone in their dullness. They share that distinction with *have, come, go, make, move,* and *get.* These common verbs do little to enliven writing. Each has so many different uses that they creep into sentences virtually unnoticed. Use them freely in contexts where they fit, of course, but stay alert for more vivid and lively substitutes.

Active Sentences

Most events in life don't just occur by themselves. Somebody does something, somebody *acts.* Hamburgers don't just get eaten. People—Julie, Paul, and Mr. Dolan—eat them. Marriages don't just happen; men and women deliberately go out and marry each other. Touchdowns don't score, jails don't just fill up, graves aren't dug, cotton isn't picked, and herring do not simply get caught and stuffed into jars. People do all these things.

> To create interest, take advantage of your readers' natural curiosity about others.

The deeds that people do register quickly on a reader's mind. To create interest in your writing, therefore, take advantage of your reader's natural curiosity about others. Always write active sentences. Even those sentences in which no specific action occurs can be written in an "active," rather than a "passive," voice.

For example, consider who performed an action in this sentence:

> Six nights a week were spent in preparation for the concert by our class.

Clearly, the class acted. More precisely, it rehearsed for a concert, but the sentence kept you waiting until the end to tell you who performed an action. Moreover, by placing "our class" at the end, the writer has been obliged to use the passive verb, *"were spent."* If you relocate "our class" to the beginning of the sentence, you suddenly activate the whole statement:

> Our class rehearsed six nights a week in preparation for the concert.

The change not only tightens and enlivens the sentence, it adds interest. You derive the same results any time you turn passive sentences into active ones:

PASSIVE

Every day, the newspaper was brought home by my father.

ACTIVE

My father brought home the newspaper every day.

PASSIVE

Rutgers was attended by my brother, my cousin, and three of my uncles.

ACTIVE

My brother, my cousin, and three uncles went to Rutgers.

Although active sentences are usually more natural, compact, and interesting, sometimes to avoid awkwardness you may need to use the passive voice. When you are uncertain who performed an action, for instance, or when it isn't important to say:

PASSIVE

The blue curtain was raised at 8:30.

ACTIVE

At 8:30, a stagehand (or Mary Ann, a production assistant) raised the curtain.

In the passive sentence curtain time is the important fact. Who pulled the rope is immaterial.

Fresh Language and Surprises

Fresh language (1) stimulates the mind, (2) pleases the ear, and (3) surprises the emotions—all praiseworthy effects of a college essay. Dull writing, on the other hand, is predictable. That is, you can almost tell what word is likely to come next in a sentence. When readers know what to expect, they'll soon lose interest, both in the writing and its author. If you serve up verbal surprises, however, your readers will stick with you.

You don't need rare or unusual words to surprise your readers. A common word, deftly used, will do:

ORDINARY

I was ten before I saw my first pigeon.

SURPRISING

I was ten before I met my first pigeon.

Since people don't normally *meet* pigeons, the unexpected shift from *saw* to *met* creates a small surprise.

ORDINARY

The shark bit the swimmers.

SURPRISING

The shark dined on the swimmers.

Changing the verb *bit* to *dined* makes a common sentence uncommon, because the word *dined* suggests good manners and gentility, pleasures that few sharks enjoy.

Sounds can create surprises, too. Some words match the sounds they describe. The word *bombard,* for example, makes a heavy, explosive sound. *Yawn* has a wide-open sound that can be stretched out indefinitely. *Choke* sticks in your throat. *Murmuring streams* evokes the sound of—what else?

> When you surprise your readers, they'll stick with you.

A reader often derives unexpected pleasure from the repetition of sounds—either consonants or vowels—as in *"The dark, dank day smelled of death"* or *"The machine sucked up the sewage in the swamp."* You probably shouldn't repeat sounds too often because they may distract the reader from the meaning of your words, but an occasional treat for the ear builds interest in your writing.

Surprise with Comparisons

It isn't easy to find just the right word to express all you think, sense and do. How, for instance, do you show the look a toll collector gave you, or how do you describe six-in-the-morning street sounds? What about the taste of stale Coke, the smell of rotting garbage, the feel of clean sheets, a fear, a frustration?

> With comparisons you can express the inexpressible.

Writers often catch those elusive details and fleeting sensations by making comparisons. An original comparison will not only delight your reader, but it will provide you with words to express your most inexpressible ideas. In addition, comparisons are economical. They require fewer words than you might otherwise need to state an idea.

To describe old men in a nursing home, for instance, you could show their creased faces, the folds of papery skin at their throats, the pale, cracked lips, and the white stubble on their chins. If you don't need all those details in your essay, you could simply compare the men to slats on weathered wooden fences. Instantly your reader will get the picture. Yes, the rough gray texture of weather-beaten boards does suggest withered men lined up in a nursing home corridor, a likeness that probably hadn't occurred to the reader before.

Small children usually don't know enough words to express all they want to say. By nature, therefore, they make comparisons: "Daddy, when my foot goes to sleep, it feels like ginger ale." As people get older, they often lose the knack and have to relearn it. When you consciously seek comparisons, though, you'll find them sprouting everywhere—like weeds. Compare, for example, the taste of fruit punch to antifreeze, a sweet look to something you'd pour on waffles, a friend's voice to a chicken's cackle, the smell of a locker room to rotting hay.

Figures of speech, such as similes (Tom wrestles *like* a tiger) and metaphors (Tom *is* a tiger), are types of comparisons. They help the writer point out likenesses between something familiar (tiger) and something unfamiliar (Tom the wrestler). One side of the comparison must always be common and recognizable. Therefore, comparing the cry of the Arctic tern to the song of a tree toad won't help a reader familiar with neither water birds nor tree toads. Since most people know what a fiddle sounds like, a more revealing comparison would be: *The cry of the Arctic tern sounds like a fiddler tuning up.*

American English is littered with hundreds of metaphors and similes, once fresh and surprising, but now dried out and lifeless. Avoid those like the plague. *"Like the plague,"* in fact, is one you should avoid. Figures of speech like *"high as a kite"* and *"pale as a ghost"* have lost their zing. Don't resurrect them in your essay. Let them rest in the cliché graveyard.

At one time, every familiar combination of words, such as *"you've got to be kidding"* and *"I couldn't care less"* was new, witty, or poetic. Such expressions were so striking that people, thinking that they would seem up to date, witty, or poetic, used them over and over. Constant use dulled them and turned them into clichés. No reader will delight in a cliché. By definition, a cliché has lost its kick.

A TREASURY OF WORTHLESS PHRASES AND EXPRESSIONS TO BE AVOIDED AT ALL COSTS

bummer	would you believe?
how does that sit with you?	go off the deep end
to touch base with	have a fit
off the top of my head	for openers
try an idea on for size	flipped out
how does that grab you?	get off my back
that's beat!	super!
far out!	so amazing
I'm getting psyched	no way

There are countless others to guard against. The number is *awesome.* They sneak into writing *when your back is turned,* when *your defenses are down,* and *when you least expect them.* Beware!

To avoid overused expressions, ask yourself whether you've ever heard or seen the phrase before. If you have, drop it, not *like a hot potato,* but just as quickly.

Sentence Variety

Monotony kills interest. A steady diet of mashed potatoes dulls the taste buds. A 200-mile stretch on a straight road takes the joy out of driving. Day after day of routine rots the brain. Listening too often to the same song destroys its charm. So it is with writing an essay. Repetition of the same sentence pattern makes readers wish they didn't have to read any further. Keep your readers awake, alert, and interested by serving up a variety of sentence patterns.

> Sentence variety keeps readers awake, alert, and interested.

Most English sentences begin with the subject, as in

> My sister got married last summer in a hot-air balloon 1,000 feet over Connecticut.

To avoid the monotony of many successive sentences in the same pattern, move the subject elsewhere and look for other ways to start a sentence:

> In a hot-air balloon 1,000 feet over Connecticut, my sister married her high school sweetheart Jack.

After an initial prepositional phrase, the writer named the subject, *"my sister."*

> Surprisingly, ten people witnessed the wedding—five in the same balloon basket, and five in another.

Obviously, the writer began this sentence with an adverb.

> When word got out about the wedding site, reporters hounded the couple for days.

After introducing this sentence with a dependent clause, the writer named the subject, *"reporters,"* and then added the rest of the sentence.

> Still, the ceremony itself was held without fanfare.

This writer snuck in the subject after an opening connective.

> To keep the wedding quiet, Jack and Annie kept the date to themselves until the night before the flight.

To compose the sentence, the writer began with a *verbal,* in this instance the infinitive form of the verb *keep.* Verbals look and feel like verbs, but aren't. At least they're not the verbs that groups of words need to qualify as complete sentences. Verbals come from verbs, though, which explains the resemblance.

> Drinking champagne, the guests flew for an hour before landing on a par-four fairway of a golf course.

Hoping to keep the reader's interest, this writer began the sentence with another kind of verbal—a participle. Very often the *i-n-g* ending indicates that you've used a participle.

> Thrilled by the adventure, the wedding party vowed to fly again on Jack and Annie's first anniversary.

Determined to begin a sentence with another kind of verbal, the writer chose a verb with an *e-d* ending, which functions like an adjective.

Still another appealing variation is the sentence containing a paired construction. In such a sentence, you have two equal and matched ideas. Sometimes the ideas differ only by one or two words, as in: *"It wasn't that I was turning away from my family, it was my family that was turning away from me"* or *"While I put my heart into dancing, dancing worked its way into my heart."* The strength of such sentences lies in the balance of parallel parts. Each part could stand alone, but together the thought becomes memorable.

Once in a great while, you can create interest by reversing the usual order of words in a sentence. When used often the writing will sound stilted and unnatural, but look at the power you get out of a sentence that begins with an adjective that you want the reader to remember: *"Desperate I grew when the telegram hadn't arrived."* Likewise, an inverted statement—*"A math genius I am not"*—carries a lot more punch than *"I am not a math genius."* Use inverted sentences cautiously, though. In the wrong place they'll sound silly.

Lucky is the writer in search of variety, for English contains a huge selection of sentence types, many of which you probably learned about in school. Obviously, there are long and short sentences. At your fingertips you also have simple, compound, and complex sentences. You have declarative, interrogative, imperative, and exclamatory sentences. You can write sentences interrupted in midstream by a dash—although some people will tell you it's not quite proper. You can also use direct and indirect quotes, and once in a great while—to drive home a point—a single emphatic word. Perfect!

With such an array, there's no excuse for writing humdrum sentences that march monotonously through your essay. Please your reader with combinations and variations. Don't mix up sentence types just to mix up sentence types, however. You may end up with a mess on your hands. Always be guided by what seems clearest and by what seems varied enough to hold your reader's interest.

A NOTE ON REPETITION

On occasion, skillful use of repetition enables you to stress an idea in an unusual way. At first glance, for example, this passage from Sally McC's essay appears repetitive:

> My grandmother raised me. She took pride in her five grandchildren. She introduced me to theater and ballet. She sat patiently through my piano and dance recitals. She sent me to sleep-away camp every summer. She did all a mother is expected to do except live long enough to see me applying to Smith, her alma mater.

Every sentence but the first starts with the same word. Yet, the paragraph isn't monotonous. What strikes you is not the similarity of the sentences, but the grandmother's devotion to child rearing. In this instance, Sally used repetition to her advantage.

Short and Long Sentences

Sentences come in all lengths, from one word to thousands. A long sentence demands greater effort from readers because, while stepping from one part of the sentence to the next, they must keep track of more words, modifiers, phrases (not to speak of parenthetical asides), and clauses without losing the writer's main thought, which may be buried amid any number of secondary, or less important, thoughts.

A balance of short and long sentences works best.

Short sentences are easier to grasp. A brief sentence makes its point quickly and sometimes with considerable potency, as for example in this passage from Tracy P's essay about a trip to Florida:

> For a day and a night the five of us—my parents, two sisters and I—sat upright in our van and drove and drove and drove. For thirty hours we shared our thoughts and dreams, counted McDonald's, told stories, ate granola bars, drank juice, dozed, played twenty questions, sat wordlessly, and finally, by the water in Daytona, we watched a brilliant crimson sun rise out of the Atlantic. But mostly, we argued.

The brief sentence at the end jolts the reader. Its bluntness, especially after a windy, forty-two-word sentence, produces a mild shock. Placing a tight, terse sentence next to a lengthy one creates a startling effect. The technique, however, works best when used only rarely. Overuse dilutes its impact.

Also, several short sentences in a row can be as tiresome as a string of long, complex sentences. A balance works best. If you have strung together four or five equally long (or short) sentences, separate (or combine) them. Here, to illustrate, is a drawn-out sentence in need of dismemberment:

> Because I was certain that it would be all right, without waiting for the approval of my mother, who was not yet home from the hospital after her operation for a back ailment that had been troubling her for years—in fact, ever since her automobile accident on the way to Chicago on Christmas, I decided during spring vacation to apply for a job as a counselor at a summer camp for children, six to fourteen years old, in Brookdale, a tiny village close to my uncle's farm in Wisconsin.

To lighten the load of an extended sentence like this, you could divide it, rearrange it, add verbs, drop an idea or two, change the emphasis, and excise words. You could employ some of the sentence-fixing tools described on pages 106 to 109. When you're done, the ideas, now clearer and more streamlined, might sound something like this:

> During spring vacation I applied for a counselor's job at a summer camp in the tiny village of Brookdale, Wisconsin. The camp, for six- to fourteen-year-olds, is near my uncle's farm. I was certain my mother wouldn't mind. So I didn't wait for her to return from the hospital, where she was recuperating from an operation for a back ailment.

Conversely, you achieve greater balance when you combine a string of several very short sentences. For instance:

> I live in two environments. I was born in Canada. I lived there for ten years. Then we moved to Boston. That was an important event. It was painful. The kids in Boston were cold and distant. All my friends were in Montreal.

Although the terse sentences may vaguely suggest the writer's despair, the writing style calls to mind a grade school primer. Greater fluidity and grace are expected from college applicants. Therefore, a renovation of the passage is needed—perhaps something like this:

> I am from two environments, one Canadian and one American. I was born in Montreal, but moved to Boston at age 10. The move was painful. Cold and distant acquaintances surrounded me in Boston. Friends lived in Montreal.

Note that you frequently get a small bonus when you combine sentences: Your writing gets more active and less wordy—both worthy goals for a writer.

The Final Check

If you took the task of editing seriously, your essay should now be in very good shape, maybe in better shape than you are. Many writers, even the best, sometimes don't know whether their hard labor and sacrifice are worth it. They can't tell whether they've done a good job. Self-doubt is the writer's trademark, the price you pay for a clear, precise, interesting, and correct essay.

Although your essay may half-sicken you by now, stick with it just a little longer. It's probably better than you think. After all, you're not a professional writer so you shouldn't expect to write like one. High school quarterbacks don't play for the Dallas Cowboys, high school actors don't win Emmys, and high school writers—even the best of them—can't compete with the professionals. Chances are you've written a decent essay that will stand up in any college admissions office. Your struggle to get the words right has probably paid off. You've revised and edited, re-revised and re-edited. Good! You added, cut, switched parts around. Very good! That shows you've been thinking. You used up lots of paper. You walked away, came back, tried again. Perhaps you wrote ten times as many words as you actually used.

Finally, you got the words the way you wanted them—the way they should be. You survived the ordeal, and the reader in the admissions office, who doesn't know you yet—but soon will—will be happy to make your acquaintance.

Before you type the finished copy of your essay, check the whole thing one more time. Don't be satisfied until you can answer YES! to all the questions on this Editing Checklist:

	YES!	MOSTLY	HARDLY	NO
Does the essay *sound* like you?	❏	❏	❏	❏
Have you used *plain* words?	❏	❏	❏	❏
Have you used *exact* language?	❏	❏	❏	❏
Does your essay have *focus*?	❏	❏	❏	❏
Are all parts in *harmony*?	❏	❏	❏	❏
Is each sentence *accurately* worded?	❏	❏	❏	❏
Have you *trimmed* needless words?	❏	❏	❏	❏
Do you *show* more than *tell*?	❏	❏	❏	❏
Have you used *active verbs*?	❏	❏	❏	❏
Is your language *fresh*?	❏	❏	❏	❏
Do you include verbal *surprises*?	❏	❏	❏	❏
Are your sentences *varied*?	❏	❏	❏	❏
Is sentence length *balanced*?	❏	❏	❏	❏

6 PRESENTING *YOUR* ESSAY

Appearance

Would you like to hear a sad but true story? It's about Scott, a high school senior, a good student with a keen desire to go to Oberlin. He wrote his essay with care but sent it in looking as though it had been kicking around in his locker for weeks. Scott was rejected. The admissions people concluded that Scott couldn't be seriously interested in Oberlin if he submitted such a sloppy-looking piece of work.

Obviously, there's a lesson in Scott's tale: Don't send in an essay that looks anything less than gorgeous.

> Your essay's appearance speaks for you as clearly as its content.

Present your essay with pride, as close to perfect as you can make it. It should be neat, crisp, and, above all, easy to read. Unless the college asks for an essay written in your own hand, as Brown University does, write it on a computer using 12-point or 10-point type—nothing smaller. Use an ordinary font like Times or Garamond, similar to the print in this book. Avoid exotic fonts like Vivaldi and Pristina. They may look pretty but cannot be read easily. Double-spaced or 1.5-spaced text is preferable to single-space. Katie Fretwell, the Amherst College director of admission, observes "Admission committees are not likely to award 'extra credit' for fancy fonts or perfect calligraphy, nor are demerits distributed for the old-fashioned hand-written essay—as long as it is legible." University of Vermont's admission associate Susan Wertheimer urges students to prepare distraction-free essays. "Fancy graphics, tiny fonts to compress lots of text onto one page, or large fonts to use up space are often mere annoyances," she says. "You *do* want your essay to stand out but not for the wrong reasons."

Use high-quality white paper, 8½ by 11 inches. If the application leaves space for written responses, it is perfectly fine to print your words on a computer, then neatly trim the sheet and attach it to the application. But adhere to the instructions. Guidelines such as "Use only the space provided" should be taken seriously. So should word limits. Colleges mean business when they say write 250 words. (MIT says "Yes, we'll count.") For most other colleges, though, its permissible to go over or under by, say, ten percent. Too many words (or too few) will count against you. If no limits or guidelines are given, consider the following: Admissions officials must read scores of essays every day. They don't have time to read lengthy, rambling essays. They want a quick take on who you are and what you value. Give it to them as succinctly as possible. An excellent rule of thumb is that two double-spaced, typewritten pages is the absolute maximum. One and a half pages is even better.

To make the presentation of your essay clear and legible, place your text in the middle of the page, leaving at least a one-inch margin all around. Number your pages, and if you are asked to write more than one essay, designate which is which by using the question number or topic from the application.

It goes without saying that cross-outs and last-minute insertions using arrows, asterisks, paragraph markers, or carets are not acceptable. Don't change anything on your final copy unless you are prepared to reprint it. Aim to make your essay letter-perfect. In all respects, neatness counts. Heed the words of Margaret Drugovich, Vice President of Admission at Ohio Wesleyan University: "Hard-to-read essays can be very annoying," she says, "and probably affect the reader's perception of the overall quality of a student's application."

Proofreading

To proofread well, you need fresh eyes. Therefore, your best proofreading method is to let someone else do it. Photocopy five copies of your essay, and have five reliable readers scour your piece for flaws in grammar, punctuation, and spelling.

If you're on your own, put your essay aside for a few days, if possible. Then read your essay slowly, once for the sense of it and once for mechanics. Read it a line at a time, keeping a hawklike watch on every letter, word, and mark of punctuation. You might even cut a narrow horizontal window out of a spare sheet of paper.

> Read your essay slowly, once for the sense of it and once for the mechanics.

Move the window over your essay a line at a time, concentrating on that line only. Search for missing words, extra words, and flawed grammar and punctuation.

Use the grammar and spell checker on your computer, but remember that the computer won't detect misused words or words that sound alike but take different spellings: *there, their,* and *they're; its* and *it's; to, two,* and *too.* Also, such words as *principal* and *principle, stationary* and *stationery, whether* and *weather,* and dozens of others that trap unwary writers. Students using the Common Application face another potential pitfall, according to the dean of admissions at Denison University, Perry Robinson: "They send the same essay to more than one college and forget to change the name of the college in their essays." Imagine the reaction of a reader in the Denison admissions office discovering that the applicant had "always wanted to go to Colgate."

Getting Help

Since you began your essay, it's likely that you've shown drafts to people you trust—good friends, a parent, teacher, advisor, or college counselor. When you're facing a tough new assignment like writing a college essay, it's natural to seek a word of encouragement or help. Indeed, you're lucky to know people who will help. If you're willing to pay for help, go to the Internet. Numerous sites offer editorial assistance for fees ranging from fifty to several hundred dollars, depending on the number and length of the essays and the type of service you ask for. Getting help from others, though, raises the impossible ethical question: When does your work cease to be yours and become theirs? There's a thin boundary between help and meddling. With luck, your well-meaning helpers haven't overstepped it.

> It's immoral and dangerous to submit an essay that cannot honestly be called yours.

If you've received suggestions for rewording a sentence or two, changing a few words, or clarifying an idea, you are probably still master of your own essay. If the help consisted of extensive rewriting, bloodying your paper with a river of red ink, and putting words in your mouth, you're about to submit an essay that cannot honestly be called yours. This is not only immoral, it's dangerous.

Books like this one feature essays that worked. Let them inspire you. Sample essays are often published by newspapers and magazines. By all means, read them, and let them trigger ideas for you to write about. Online web sites offer essays for sale or for the taking. With so many model essays at their fingertips, some students can't resist the temptation to lift all or part of an essay they didn't write, submit it, and hope for the best. Jonathan Reider, Senior Associate Director of Admission at Stanford, says, "You'd be surprised by how many copied essays we see. We once had two essays on dance that were clearly copied from the same source. To this day, we don't know what the source was, but we knew the essays were too similar to have been written by accident. We never would have noticed if we had received only one, but since we got two, both applicants were doomed."

Moreover, people who read college essays for a living know the distinctive style of high school writing. Even the best of it differs from the writing of adults. Perhaps it's the rhythm, the use of a certain word, an unusual turn of phrase, the juxtaposition of ideas—each can tip off a reader that an adult has had a hand in the essay. There are certain usages that, although natural for an experienced adult writer, would almost never find their way into a high school student's essay. (The sentence you just read contains just such an example. Notice that the subordinate clause, "although natural for an experienced adult writer," is embedded in the main clause. One in a thousand high school writers is likely to construct a sentence like that. It would be equally rare, too, for a high school student to say "usages . . . find their way." Teenagers don't express themselves that way.)

That's not to say that every ably written application essay will arouse suspicion in the admissions office. Many applicants write superior essays all by themselves. If a student with average English grades and unexceptional College Board scores submits a slick, highly sophisticated essay, however, a reader will notice. When admissions officers have reason to question the authorship of an essay, they'll scrutinize the applicant's school record and search through teachers' recommendations for mention of the student's writing ability. If they still have doubts, they may phone the high school for verification.

Getting substantial help with an essay may reduce your anxiety, but it also does you a disservice. You should make it into the college of your choice based on what you know, what you can do, and who you are. Misrepresenting yourself may get you in, but once on campus *you* will do the work, *you* will do the writing, *you* will sink or swim on your own. An essay that fools the admissions office will grant you a short-lived victory. In a few months, the real you will start bringing home real grades. Your application essay will be history, as will, perhaps, your career as a student at that college.

In Addition to Your Essay

Some colleges want more than an essay from you. They ask for paragraph-long responses to any number of questions—why you chose that particular college, which extracurricular activity you like the most, your favorite book, career plans, honors, and so on. Whatever your answers, write them with the same care as your essay. Start with drafts. Revise and edit. Use your most interesting writing style. Since you're usually limited to less than half a dozen lines, get to the point promptly and express yourself concisely. Be attentive to the sound and style of your responses.

Some questions invite you to reply with a list of some kind—travels, prizes, alumni connections. If you can, however, respond with a thoughtful, well-developed paragraph. Not only will your answer be more interesting to read, you'll have the opportunity to emphasize the items that matter. Moreover, the reader will note that you took the trouble to write a coherent, lucid paragraph and that your writing repertoire contains more than just a college essay.

When an application asks, "Is there additional information we should know?" try to reply with an emphatic "Yes!" Since your essay won't have told them everything, grab this chance to explain more of yourself or to show your interests and accomplishments. Applicants frequently send their creative work—perhaps a short story, a collection of poetry, articles written for the school paper, slides of artwork, photographs—almost anything that fits into an envelope or small package. Don't overdo it, though. One carefully chosen term paper will suffice to reveal your love of history. One chapter of your novel is more than admissions people will have time to read, anyway. Quality, not quantity, counts.

Whatever you send, prepare it with the same high standards you used on your essay. Written material should be typed; photographs and artwork should be attractively displayed and clearly explained or captioned. Before you mail a tape of your music or a video of your gymnastic performance, wind it to the starting point. Make certain that it works and that it contains only what you want the college to hear or see. Also, submit only a few minutes' worth of material—not your whole concert or routine.

Don't feel obliged to create a piece of work just for your college application. Most people don't. It's not their style. Furthermore, most admissions officials realize that high school seniors have enough to do without the burden of an additional project. But if you have something on hand that reveals your uniqueness, by all means use it. For example, a girl interested in photography sent to Ohio Wesleyan a tasteful male pin-up calendar that she and a friend had marketed. A Tufts applicant sent copies of the school literary magazine she had edited. A young man who makes and sells intricate metal puzzles explained to the colleges why he sent one with each of his applications—"something to keep you entertained while reading essays." Two friends, both applying to Columbia, sent in a movie they had made together. One aspiring architect submitted his blueprints for a geodesic-domed city with his MIT application. The Northwestern admissions office received a poem written on a jigsaw puzzle. To read the poem, the puzzle had to be assembled. It's not clear, however, whether it was ever completed.

> Don't go too far trying to be clever. Being yourself is your best bet.

Be creative, of course. Be serious if you're serious, witty if you're witty. Just don't go too far trying to be clever. Being yourself is your best bet.

Your Friend, the Mail Carrier

What a glorious feeling it will be to click the "send" button on your computer or turn your application and essay over to the U.S. Postal Service. Then sit back and rejoice. Pat yourself on the back for a job well done. Relax and wait for the momentous day when the mail carrier brings you the *fat* envelope—the one containing information about housing, courses, freshman orientation, and, of course, the letter that begins, "It gives me great pleasure to tell you that you have been accepted in the class of. . . ."

APPENDIX A.
ESSAY TOPICS FROM OVER
FIFTY POPULAR COLLEGES

American University (Choose one)

1. Imagine you are the editor of a major national news magazine. Write the cover story you would choose for the issue that would be on the newsstands January 1, 2010.
2. Describe an event or individual that has been instrumental in shaping who you are. Tell us why this event/person has been significant in your life.
3. Instead of writing on one of the above topics, you may submit a creative/fiction writing sample completed for a class.

Amherst (Two essays)

Two essays from the Common Application. In lieu of one of them, choose the following supplementary essay: Select a short test, a formula or a visual image written or created by someone other than yourself. Respond to it. Limit: 500 words.

Bard (Two essays)

1. Write an essay on a personal, local, or national issue that is of particular concern to you.
2. Discuss your intellectual development and how it relates to your interest in attending college, particularly Bard. Refer to an individual, an author, a book or an intellectual or aesthetic experience that was instrumental in your intellectual development and college plans.

Barnard

The members of the Committee on Admissions seek to gain an understanding of you as a person. This essay is your opportunity to discuss an idea that matters to you, to write about a person who has influenced you, or to describe an experience that has helped shape who you are. The Committee is also interested in how you think and how you express your thoughts.

Bennington (Choose two)

1. Mary Oliver teaches literature and writing at Bennington College. In 1983, she won the Pulitzer Prize for her sixth book of poems, *American Primitive.* This is a poem from her 1990 collection, *House of Light:*

The Summer Day

Who made the world?
Who made the swan, and the black bear?
Who made the grasshopper?
This grasshopper, I mean—
the one who has flung herself out of the grass,
the one who is eating sugar out of my hand,
who is moving her jaws back and forth instead of up and down—
who is gazing around with her enormous and complicated eyes.
Now she lifts her pale forearms and thoroughly washes her face.
Now she snaps her wings open, and floats away.
I don't know exactly what a prayer is.
I do know how to pay attention, how to fall down
into the grass, how to kneel down in the grass,
how to be idle and blessed, how to stroll through the fields,
which is what I have been doing all day.
Tell me, what else should I have done?
Doesn't everything die at last, and too soon?
Tell me, what is it you plan to do
with your wild and precious life?

Write about something that you think is worth paying attention to. It does not have to be a creature that lives in the grass; it might be a person who works at the store on the corner, or the manner in which your grandmother answers questions—or any other subject that you find fascinating.

2. Design an experiment that attempts to determine whether toads can hear. Provide the rationale for your design—explain your reasons for setting up the experiment as you did. Strive for simplicity and clarity. (Betsy Sherman, a biologist at Bennington, uses this question to invite her students to discover

the difficulties and pleasures of investigating how animals work.)

   There are many imaginative ways to approach this problem; you do *not* need to be a scientist or do any special research in order to respond.

3. Donald Sherefkin, a teacher of architecture at Bennington, recently assigned the following project to students in his "Introduction to Architecture" course. Please respond to it using words, drawings, models, or some combination of the three.

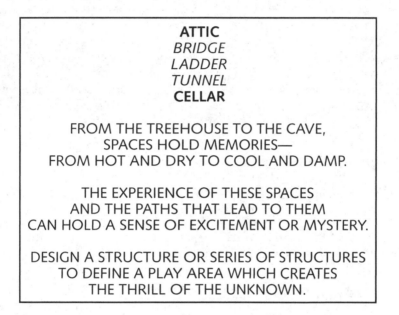

ATTIC
BRIDGE
LADDER
TUNNEL
CELLAR

FROM THE TREEHOUSE TO THE CAVE,
SPACES HOLD MEMORIES—
FROM HOT AND DRY TO COOL AND DAMP.

THE EXPERIENCE OF THESE SPACES
AND THE PATHS THAT LEAD TO THEM
CAN HOLD A SENSE OF EXCITEMENT OR MYSTERY.

DESIGN A STRUCTURE OR SERIES OF STRUCTURES
TO DEFINE A PLAY AREA WHICH CREATES
THE THRILL OF THE UNKNOWN.

4. Design a question that could reveal an important aspect of who you are. Write the question and your response to it.

Boston University

Write an essay of no more than 500 words on any subject that interests you. For example, you may choose to write on an issue about which you feel strongly, an experience that has greatly influenced your life, or other circumstances that you would like the Admissions staff to consider in reviewing your application. These are only suggestions, however; the choice of topic is yours.

Brown

Your personal essay should be just what we consider it to be—your opportunity to tell us about anything you think we should know. Personal essays vary greatly from application to application in terms of form and content. Some students choose to write poems and/or songs for their essays. Many relate especially thought-provoking experiences or personal relationships. The personal statement is your opportunity to introduce us to you and to educate us about those personal aspects which you determine are vital for us to know. We ask only that whatever you write be honestly written and in your own handwriting. Incidentally, there is only one wrong essay— it's entitled, "Why I Want to Go to Brown." While that topic may have great literary value, it tells us about Brown—a subject about which we know a good deal, and not about you—a subject about which we know very little. One final suggestion—don't wait until the last day to complete the question. We know you have better things to do on New Year's Eve than to compose your Brown essay.

Carnegie-Mellon

One Common Application question
> OR

How do you think your participation in service to others might influence your future academic or career plans?

Case Western Reserve

A required writing sample that should demonstrate your best possible work and offer insight into you as a person. Rather than require you to write yet another college essay, you may choose to submit work on which you have already spent quality time. . . . Suggestions include an essay you prepared for another college application, a personal statement, or other creative effort that provides insight into your personality. *Not recommended: original poetry, literary criticism, research papers, etc.*

Colby College (Choose two)

1. We are committed to building a community. We ask you to write an essay that will help us understand your thoughts and feelings about people who are genuinely concerned about the rights

and freedoms of others. Please keep in mind your potential contribution to this campus community as you write on this topic.
*Racial, ethnic, and religious divisions continue to trouble society.
Based on your own experience, what hopes and fears do you hold
for the future?*
2. Each of us comes from a unique background. Tell us how yours
has been shaped as you write on this topic. *Describe your home-
town.*
3. More than 70 percent of Colby students study abroad at some
point in their college careers. These broadening experiences lead
to a heightened awareness on campus of global issues and to
intense discussion about them. *Discuss a global issue of particular importance to you.*
4. The power of words to influence and persuade underlies much of
what the liberal arts contribute to society. At Colby we consider
seriously the ways in which words shape us. *What have you
read that has caused you to change significantly the way you see
the world or some aspect of it—and perhaps, even, to alter how
you live your life?*

Columbia

Write an essay which conveys to the reader a sense of who you are.
Possible topics may include, but are not limited to, experiences
which have shaped your life, the circumstances of your upbring-
ing, the way you see the world—the people in it, events great and
small, everyday life—or any personal theme which appeals to your
imagination. Please remember that we are concerned not only
with the substance of your prose but with your writing style as
well. Though it is not required, we prefer that you limit yourself to
the space provided.

Cornell (Choose one)

1. Think about something you never did in high school but wish
you had done. Now imagine your time at Cornell. Propose taking up something daring and new, and describe how it might
affect your life.
2. "A stone, a leaf, an unfound door." *Look Homeward, Angel,*
Thomas Wolfe. Write about three objects that would give the
admissions selection committee insight into who you are.
3. On rereading his personal journals in the last few years of his
life, E. B. White, author, journalist, and Cornell graduate (1921)

wrote: "Where I would like to discover facts, I find fancy. Where I would like to learn what I did, I learn only what I was thinking. They are loaded with opinion, moral thoughts, quick evaluations, youthful hopes and cares and sorrows. Occasionally, they manage to report something in exquisite honesty and accuracy. That is why I have refrained from burning them."

Please write a page from your own life journal that reports something in "exquisite honesty and accuracy."

Dartmouth

Please feel free to convey anything significant that you think we should know. This could be an anecdote or essay related to an interest, talent, experience, issue of concern, or aspect of your background or qualifications. Anything goes!

Duke

Two required short answers (a and b)
   a. Why do you consider Duke a good match for you? Is there something in particular you anticipate contributing to the Duke community? If you are applying to the School of Engineering, you may discuss your interest in the field of engineering in general or your interest in Duke's program specifically.
   b. Consider the books you have read in the last year or two either for school or for leisure. Please discuss the way in which one of them changed your understanding of the world, other people, or yourself.
Also one of the following essay questions:
   c. According to Stephen Carter, we can admire those with integrity even if we disagree with them. Are there people you admire even though you deeply disagree with them? What do you admire about them? How do you reconcile this apparent contradiction in your assessment?
   d. What has been your most profound or surprising intellectual experience?
   e. Please write on a matter of importance to you. Any topic, and any form of written expression, is acceptable. If you have written something for another purpose—even an essay for another college—that you believe represents you particularly well, feel free to submit it here. As a guideline, remember that we are especially interested in issues of personal significance.

Emory

Please choose a subject of genuine interest to you. In the past we have been delighted and educated by candidates' topics. They have written about personal aspirations, travel experiences, family situations, national events, people who have influenced them, significant experiences, and some have just used their imaginations. There is no right or wrong response to this request. In writing about something that is of interest to you, you will express more about yourself. Good writing can address any topic.

George Washington (Choose one)

1. *Leave your mark—Design a question:* If our choices fail to inspire you, here is your chance to influence our Admissions Committee as well as demonstrate your ability at writing. Develop an essay question and justify why you would support its inclusion in GW's application for admission. Evaluate your proposed question and advocate for your position. For example, consider these approaches in your development: How is your question germane to GW? To our location in Washington, D.C.? What academic or personal qualities in the applicant would your question reveal that would otherwise be unexplored? Why would Admissions Officers be interested in reading such an essay response? What does your question say to the applicant about GW? (Your essay question becomes the property of the GW Admissions Office and may appear in future publications—don't be surprised if it is yours!)
2. *Design Your Own Monument:* (Case in point: The Vietnam Veteran's Memorial designed by college student Maya Lin Ying, who at age 21 was commissioned to design the memorial after competing nationally for the honor.) Now it is your turn to immortalize a movement, an event, a person, a generation, an icon. *What would your national monument commemorate or celebrate?* What materials or medium would you choose? Where in Washington, D.C., would you locate your memorial? What engraved words or music would further convey the symbolism of your tribute? (Illustrations are welcome.)
3. In lieu of responding to one of the above questions, you may choose to submit a *graded* creative/fiction writing sample. No term papers please.

Hamilton (Choose one)

1. Why are you excited about science, and how could you imagine using your knowledge of science to benefit society?
2. What poem, play, book, or painting, symphony, dance or other work of art has affected you deeply in the last two years, and why?
3. Briefly describe an important problem in the global community or in contemporary American society. What conditions, changes or events have caused this problem?
4. Describe a significant experience or achievement that has special meaning to you.

Hampshire (Two essays)

1. Personal Statement
   You may wish to write about a significant academic or personal experience and how it has shaped our outlook; a person who has had a particular influence on your life; a risk you have taken or a challenge you have faced; or how you imagine your future. If you have experienced a specific problem that has affected your academic performance, please address this in your statement.
2. Analytic Essay (Submit one of the following)
   a. An academic paper you have written for a class in the past year, including your teacher's grade and comments. Please attach a note indicating the course for which the paper was written, the date, and the nature of the assignment.
   b. An analytic essay on any of the topics below or on a similarly complex question of your own design:
      • Discuss a local, national, or international issue of your choice in an analytic manner. Are there possibilities for change available? What obstacles do you see to constructive change? What factors are most important in understanding this issue?
      • Submit a copy of an article on a significant topic and critique it. Are there facts, arguments, or points of view that the writer has failed to acknowledge? Do you agree or disagree with the author, and why? If the author suggests an outcome or course of action, does he or she anticipate the effect?
      • Compare two works of art from the same or different media that convey similar ideas or approaches, or that stem from the same movement (i.e., expressionist poetry

and painting or baroque architecture and music.) Analyze what the artists convey, how they have used the medium. Have they been effective?

- Science will play a crucial role in such critical issues as the AIDS crisis, environmental destruction, health care, and world hunger. Support for science-based research and policy analysis are often influenced by culture, religion, gender, economics, or politics. Describe such an issue, the complex forces and play, and your recommendations.

Harvard

Common Application and optional supplemental essay. Possible topics: unusual circumstances of your life, travel or living experiences in other countries, books that have affected you most, an academic experience (course, project, paper, or research topic) that has meant the most to you, a list of books you have read during the past twelve months.

Haverford

We want to know you better. Please write an essay in which you describe an especially meaningful experience, accomplishment, or personal quality of yours. Tell us something about yourself that the other application materials have not covered.

Although we want you to be concise, we do not wish to limit your creativity or stifle your voice; the length of your essay is less important than your message.

Holy Cross (Choose one)

1. It is the morning of your high school graduation day. Write a letter to the person you were freshman year, reflecting upon all the lessons you have learned throughout your high school career.
2. The late artist Andy Warhol once said that "in the future, everyone will be world-famous for fifteen minutes." What events do you imagine will lead to **your** "fifteen minutes of fame" in life?
3. What is your definition of "the good life?"

Ithaca College

Select a topic of personal, local, national, or international concern and explain why it is important to you.

Johns Hopkins (Choose one)

1. "The house of the soul," "a musical instrument," and "machine" are three examples of the many metaphors that are often employed to describe the human body. Write an essay in which you examine how the use of the metaphors affects the ways in which we study human life, see our bodies, take care of ourselves and others, or define health. Be sure to include and explain your own metaphor for the human body.
2. At Hopkins, a political science professor uses contemporary fiction by African authors to teach about the politics of southern Africa. If you were to design a course around the music, art, film, or literature that you like, what would that course be about? What would you hope to teach your students? Please include a listening/viewing/reading list with your essay.
3. Using a piece of wire, a Hopkins car window sticker, an egg carton, and any inexpensive hardware store item, create something that would solve a problem. Tell us about your creation, but don't worry; we won't require proof that it works!
4. Choose a person or an event that has been important in your life and describe in detail what makes the person or event significant to you.
5. Undergraduate study at Hopkins is distinguished by an emphasis on research and discovery as a means of learning. Art history majors, English majors, and biomedical engineering majors alike have conducted independent research in topics ranging from howler monkeys to the poetry of the inner city. Many projects are funded by grants awarded each year by our Provost's Undergraduate Research Committee. If you were applying for such a grant, what kind of research or independent study would you like to conduct? How would you outline your proposed process of inquiry to the committee?

Kenyon

The essay is your opportunity to show us who you are. It helps us see you as an individual, to understand how you think and write and what you value. With this in mind, please discuss your feelings about or reaction to some special interest, experience, achievement, or other personal issue you would like us to know about. Be creative, original, witty, serious; but most of all, be yourself.

Lafayette (Choose one)

1. Ask and answer the one question that you wish we had asked.
2. Please relate an anecdote about yourself that reveals something about your character and personal values.
3. Describe a decision that you have made and would like to make over again.

Marietta (Choose one)

1. Identify a person or an experience that has had a significant influence on the formation of your values.
2. It has been said that high school is "four years of being misunderstood." What do you think?
3. Respond to the statement, "We do not read great books, they read us."
4. In lieu of one of the above questions, you may submit a graded paper from your 11th or 12th grade English class (3 or more pages).

Marlboro

The Autobiographical Statement should help us gain an understanding of you as a person. Please tell us something more about yourself that would help us toward a sense of who you are, how you think, and what issues and ideas interest you the most.

Optional family statement to be written by parent or guardian: In our endeavor to assemble a complete portrait of each applicant to Marlboro, we ask families for comments only they can make about their children. Please offer an assessment of your child's strengths and weaknesses, emotional and intellectual character, and comment on his or her appropriateness for Marlboro.

MIT (Answer three)

1. In 100 words or less (yes, we will count), what interests you most intellectually? Why? Why are you good at it?

2. In 100 words or less (yes, we will count), what interests you extracurricularly? Why? Why are you good at it?
3. Choose one of the following for a 500-word essay:
   a. Tell us about an opinion that you have had to defend or an incident in your life which placed you in conflict with the beliefs of a majority of people and explain how this affected your value system.
   b. Make up a question that is personally relevant to you, state it clearly, and answer it. Feel free to use your imagination, recognizing that those who read it will not mind being entertained.

Northwestern (Choose one)

1. Is there something unusual that you plan to bring with you to college? (Sorry, no pets allowed.) Explain why you have it and why it is so unusual.
2. Anatole France said, "If 50 million people say a foolish thing, it is still a foolish thing." On what subject do you disagree with most people, and why?
3. What work of art or popular culture today, widely known or obscure, will be remembered 100 years from today as a representative example of taste at the end of the 20th century? What do you like or dislike about the work you have chosen?
4. Imagine you have written a short story, film, or play about your last four years. Briefly describe a defining moment or scene and how it affects the rest of your autobiographical piece.

Oberlin (Choose one)

1. A personal trait, interest, or goal, and how it reflects who you are.
2. An experience that has deeply affected you.
3. A person you admire.
4. A change you have gone through and how it may affect your future.
5. A value you hold: how it developed and why it is important to you.

Princeton (Four half-page essays)

1. What one class, teacher, book, or experience can you point to as having really *changed the way you think?* Explain.

2. Discuss something (*anything*) you just wished you understood better.
3. If you could hold one position, elected or appointed, in government (at any level), which one would you want it to be, and why?
4. What one or two suggestions would you have if asked about how we might improve race relations in this country or around the world?

Reed (Choose one)

1. Comment on an experience that helped you discern or define a value that you hold.
2. To complete this application Reed has asked for information about your personal and academic life. If you were an admission counselor, which parts of the application would carry the greatest weight as you decide who should be admitted? Explain why.
3. Answer any one of the essay questions from the Common Application.

Rensselaer Polytechnic Institute

Candidates for dental, law, physician-scientist, podiatric programs: State your reasons for aspiring to a career in dentistry, law, medicine, or podiatry.

Candidates for architecture programs: State your reasons for choosing architecture/building science as your profession.

Candidates for other programs: Choose one topic listed below.
1. Describe a significant experience or achievement that has special meaning to you.
2. Indicate a person who has had a significant influence on you, and describe that influence.
3. "They'll say I impacted the 21st century by my work in . . ."

Rochester Institute of Technology (Choose one)

1. Write a brief essay indicating your main reasons for applying to RIT.
2. Write a brief essay describing a significant experience or achievement that has special meaning for you.
3. Provide a copy of an essay you have already written for a school assignment (any subject).

Sarah Lawrence

Common Application questions plus a supplement containing two short-answer questions and an academic paper based on research and analysis that provides the admissions committee an example of the level of academic work you are doing and how it is evaluated. Teachers' remarks must be on the paper.

Stanford (Choose one)

1. How has the place in which you live influenced the person you are? Define "place" any way you like . . . as a context, a country, a city, a community, a house, a point in time.
2. Traditions are an integral part of our lives. Tell us about a tradition that is honored by your family, your friends, or your culture (or describe one that you would like to create) and talk about why it is or would be important.

Swarthmore

Please write an essay that tells us more about you. You may want to write about people who have influenced you, situations that have shaped you, difficulties or conflicts with which you have struggled, goals and hopes you may have for the future, or something else you consider significant. . . . Length should not exceed two pages.

Tulane

Write an essay describing in detail some special interest, significant experience or achievement, or anything else that has special meaning to you or has had a significant influence on you. (Recommended length: one to two pages)

University of California (Berkeley, Davis, Irvine, Los Angeles, Riverside, San Diego, Santa Barbara, Santa Cruz) Two-page essay on one or more of these topics:

1. The University seeks to enroll on each of its campuses an entering class that is academically superior and that embodies a wide range of talents, experiences, achievements and points of view. Describe the qualities and accomplishments you would

bring to the undergraduate student body at the University of California.

2. Intellectual vitality is an important value of university life. Describe one of your intellectual achievements—such as a paper, project, production or performance. Explain not only the achievement, but what you gained from it, as well.

3. It is important for the University to understand the context of each applicant's accomplishments, both academic and nonacademic. Describe any unusual circumstances or challenges you have faced and discuss the ways you have responded.

University of Chicago (Choose one)

1. *Landscape is a slippery word. It means more than scenery painting, a pleasant vista, or ornamental planting around a country house. It means shaped land, land modified for permanent human occupation, for dwelling, agriculture, manufacturing, government, worship, and for pleasure.*—John R. Stilgoe, *Common Landscapes of America*, 1580–1845.

   In light of Stilgoe's definition of landscape, think about the landscape (or cityscape) in which you live. In an essay, tell us how this landscape defines and is defined by you and your community. How does it reflect on the society in which you live? How has the landscape changed or been altered since you've lived in it?

2. Having observed the recent success of television shows about young people, the University of Chicago has decided to pitch a pilot proposal to the networks. That is as much as we are sure of now, so we are taking this opportunity to get help from the intended audience: you.

   In the tradition of the University of Chicago school of improvisation and its offshoot, the Second City comedy troupe, help us out by creating a story for your proposal. Remember that this is Chicago, so it is better to err on the side of intellectual pretension than on the side of pure silliness. Please bear in mind that *Felicity* has already been done.

   The setting is near a grand college campus—green, leafy, and gothic—in a major Midwestern city. Incorporate into your story:

   1. a genre from the following: (a) a German opera, (b) a soap opera, (c) *Real World*, (d) *Bill Nye the Science Guy*, or (e) . . . ok . . . *Friends*.

   2. a character from the following: (a) Godot, (b) Enrico Fermi's personal trainer, (c) a starving investment banker, or (d) an evil clown.

3. a prominent prop from the following: (a) Cliff's Notes for *Finnegan's Wake,* (b) van Gogh's ear, (c) a proton accelerator, or (d) Muddy Waters' guitar.

Keep your proposal to two or three pages. We know that Aristotle is out of fashion, but including a beginning, middle, and end might help you structure the story.

3. The late-eighteenth-century popular philosopher and cultural critic Georg Lichtenberg wrote, "Just as we outgrow a pair of trousers, we outgrow acquaintances, libraries, principles, etc. . . . at times before they're worn out and at times—and this is the worst of all—before we have new ones."

Write an essay about something you have outgrown, perhaps before you had a replacement—a friend, a political philosophy, a favorite author, or anything that has had an influence on you. What, if anything, has taken its place?

4. Pose a question of your own, the answer to which you believe will display your best qualities as a writer, thinker, visionary, social critic, sage, sensible woman or man, citizen of the world, or future citizen of the University of Chicago.

University of Connecticut

Include an essay to help the Admissions Office gain a more complete impression of you and what you can contribute to the University of Connecticut.

University of Maine

Please complete a statement regarding your academic goals and objectives, or an essay on a subject of personal choice.

University of Miami (Choose one)

Common Application topics or: Explain the role that academic integrity has played in your life.

University of Michigan

Submit a one-page personal essay that will help us learn more about you, what is important to you, and why, and what you hope to accomplish through a college education. You may emphasize an educational goal or an important milestone in your life. Please do not list your activities or accomplishments in this essay. If you are admitted and enroll, your academic advisor will read your essay. The essay will be used to help your advisor to become acquainted with you and to assist you in your educational planning.

University of North Carolina at Chapel Hill (Choose one)

1. Drawing on your family's experiences and your personal circumstances, tell us what you would like us to know about you that you have not already been able to tell us.
2. Provide a creative writing sample that is in some way autobiographical.

University of Pennsylvania (Choose one)

1. You have just completed your 300-page autobiography. Please submit page 217.
2. First experiences can be defining. Cite a first experience that you have had and explain its impact on you.
3. Recall an occasion when you took a risk that you now know was the right thing to do.

University of Vermont

Short essays (All required)
1. What experiences or circumstances have influenced your academic performance?
2. How have your academic interests developed? How do you plan to further those interests in college and beyond?
3. UVM supports a diverse and involved student body. What contributions might you make to our campus community outside of academic achievement?

Extended essay (Choose one)
1. Select a person you admire or a significant life experience. In what way has this person or experience affected you?
2. If you are a non-traditional or transfer candidate, describe how your life experiences have contributed to your desire to complete your undergraduate degree.
3. Select a topic of your choice.

University of Virginia (Two essays)

A 250-word essay on one of the following:
1. Make a bold prediction about something in the year 2020 that no one else has made a bold prediction about.
2. If you could cause any one living person to change his or her mind about one thing, whom would you pick, and how would you change his or her thinking?
3. "The past isn't dead. It's not even past." So says the lawyer Gavin Stevens near the end of Faulker's *Requiem for a Nun*. To borrow Stevens' words, what small event, either from your personal history or the history of the world, is neither "dead" nor "past?"
4. Does discrimination still exist? What single experience or event has led you to this conclusion?
5. What is your favorite word, and why?
                    AND
A 500-word piece of writing on any subject you choose.

University of Wisconsin

Please use this section to provide any additional information (such as your aspirations, work experience, creative talents, factors affecting your academic record, etc.) that you would like the admission committee to know.

Vanderbilt (Two essays)

1. Please discuss your academic area of interest and the reasons you have applied to the undergraduate school(s) or college(s) you indicated.
2. Each candidate for admission possesses qualities not necessarily visible in a list of activities and achievements. We have found that an essay is often an effective vehicle to a more complete and fair understanding of a candidate for admission to Vanderbilt. We leave the choice of a topic up to you. Your essay should allow us to develop a sense of your effectiveness in written communication, and to understand more fully who you are and what you value.

William and Mary (Choose one)

1. Discuss how a particular work of music, literature, art, or a photo you enclose has inspired your life.

2. Choose a current controversial issue and build the case for both sides.
3. Describe a favorite family or community tradition, and tell why it is meaningful to you.
4. Enclose a copy of an essay you wrote for another college application, which you really enjoyed writing. Be sure to tell us what the question or assignment was.

Yale (Two essays)

1. Please write an essay about an activity or interest that has been particularly meaningful to you. We ask that you limit your response to the space below (one page).
2. Please use the space on this page to let us know something about you that we might not learn from the rest of your application. We ask that you limit your response to the space provided (one page). In the past, applicants have used this space in a great variety of ways. They have written about family situations, ethnicity or culture, school or community, events to which they have had strong reactions, people who have influenced them, significant experiences, intellectual interests, personal aspirations, or—more generally—topics that spring from the life of the imagination. There is no "correct" way to respond to the essay request. In writing about something that matters to you, you will convey to us a sense of yourself.

Common Application Questions

This personal statement helps us become acquainted with you as an individual in ways different from courses, grades, test scores, and other objective data. Please write an essay (250–500 words) on a topic of your choice or on one of the options listed below.

1. Evaluate a significant experience, achievement, or risk that you have taken and its impact on you.
2. Discuss some issue of personal, local, national, or international concern and its importance to you.
3. Indicate a person who has had a significant influence on you, and describe that influence.
4. Describe a character in fiction, a historical figure, or a creative work (as in art, music, science, etc.) that has had an influence on you and explain that influence.

APPENDIX B.
ESSAYS IN PROGRESS

En route from first to final draft, essay writers often pause to survey the progress they've made. After writing each draft, they decide whether to continue as before, alter their course or even start all over again. This appendix contains two sample essays somewhere on the journey to completion. Each draft is followed by notes on what the writer should do next. Notice that later drafts of each essay incorporate the suggestions for improvement. With more drafts, who knows—the writers may have produced essays to stir the blood of the most hard-hearted admissions dean.

Ellie E's First Draft

This essay responds to the "significant personal experience" question on the Common Application. Ellie wrote her first draft rather quickly—and it shows, as you will see:

> During an Outward Bound expedition in Minnesota I was put in several difficult situations. I never could have imagined them before. I was in front of a steep 80-degree incline and told to climb it to the top. My first reaction was, "There is no way I can do it." But I had no choice. I could not stay alone in the wilderness. My effort to climb the rock was the most ambitious I have ever done in my life. After two hours, I was up on the top.
>
> Even though I was there a short time, those two weeks were the most important of my life. My approach to life was different. In freshman and sophomore year I was put in many difficult academic situations. I was not making an effort. However, when I was in junior year, I made an effort. My motivation was greatly increased. Abilities I had never used before were now coming into use. My academic program was a challenge and I was meeting it gladly. With an open mind and a

willingness and a desire to try and learn, I enriched my knowledge and sharpened my skills.

I was in an honors English class with the name Modern European Literature. It was a large amount of work outside of class as well as in class discussion. The literature was difficult. I was taking the time and effort to read it until I fully understood it. In previous years, I would have dropped the class in which I was told I was going to learn about existentialism, a topic which I knew nothing about, and also write several analytical papers.

I was also challenged in math, which is one of my weaker areas. Math is not required for graduation, and I was against taking more than the least amount required to graduate. My strong dislike for the subject was keeping me from trying to learn it. But another part of me decided to meet the challenge. I didn't think it would be impossible if I made an effort. I soon found out that making the effort taught me the concepts, and logical thinking became easier for me.

Outward Bound also proved valuable in my employment. I was working as a waitress and a cashier. I had to interact with very demanding managers, co-workers, and customers. My patience was not unlimited. However, I could deal with the pressure and with others regardless of their personalities.

In the past year and a half I have shown that I can apply this new approach to my schoolwork and to everyday situations. Now I am ready to take on the responsibilities and challenges of college life and academics.

Notes to Ellie

—You have chosen a good topic, likely to impress a college, because it shows that you know what you are capable of once you put your mind to it.

—Maintain the premise of your piece, that is, how your experience in the Minnesota wilderness helped to transform you and change your attitude toward school and work. In fact, try to strengthen the cause/effect relationship.

—You attribute your sudden transformation to a single climbing experience up a steep hill. That is not altogether plausible. To change you so dramatically, there must have been more to the Outward Bound adventure. Try to give more details. What other things occurred during those two weeks to give you a new sense of yourself?

—Your essay has good unity. You never stray from your topic.

—A word about your writing style. Note that most of your sentences use "to-be" verbs. Enliven the writing with more active verbs, which will also tighten the prose and make it more interesting to read. Also, tie ideas together with transitional words. Finally, combine sentences. Too many simple sentences tend to give equal weight to every idea. Try to emphasize the ideas that matter most.

Ellie's Second Draft

I returned from an Outward Bound expedition in Minnesota shortly before I began my junior year. The return was difficult as I tried to apply my new confidence to my everyday life, including my education. In Minnesota I had been put into several difficult situations that I never could have imagined before. I found myself in front of a steep 80-degree incline and told to climb it to the top. My first reaction was, "There is no way I can do it," but I had no choice since I could not stay alone in the wilderness. My effort to climb the rock was the most ambitious I have ever done in my life. I struggled for two hours, sometimes almost giving up. I felt it might be better just to let myself roll down the hill and be done with it. I was encouraged by others and helped by the guide. I found the strength to go on. In the end, I stood on the top feeling like I had truly conquered the world.

Although I had been in Minnesota only a short time, those two weeks were the most important of my life. My motivation to succeed had greatly increased. Abilities I had never tested before were coming into use. My junior year in high school was a challenge and one that I gladly met. With my mind open, and a willingness and desire to learn, I enriched my knowledge and sharpened my skills.

I took an honors English class entitled Modern European Literature. It involved a large amount of work outside of class as well as in class discussion. Although the literature was often difficult, I took the time and effort to read it until I fully understood it. In previous years, I would have dropped any class in which I was told I was going to read long, hard books, learn about existentialism, a topic I knew nothing about, and also write several analytical papers.

I also challenged myself in one of my weaker areas, mathematics. Because math is not required for graduation, my strong dislike for the subject tempted me to avoid it. But another part of me decided to meet the challenge. I knew it would not be impossible if I tried. I soon found out that once I made the effort to learn the concepts, logical thinking became easier for me.

The Outward Bound experience also proved valuable in my employment. Working as a waitress and a cashier, I had to interact with very demanding managers, co-workers, and customers. My patience was not unlimited. However, I managed to deal with the pressure and work, regardless of the others' personalities.

I feel that in the past year and a half I have shown that I can apply this new self-confidence and motivation to my schoolwork and to everyday situations. Now I am ready to take on the responsibilities and challenges of college life and academics.

Notes to Ellie

—This is much better than the first draft. The connection between your climb up the steep hill and your new attitude in school is much clearer now. But it could be made even stronger and more convincing if you allude to the climb in your discussion of tough courses and work experiences.

—The paragraph on your work as a waitress and cashier is still pretty vague. Either develop that paragraph further with a brief anecdote about how you coped with pressure on the job, or drop it altogether.

—Keep trying to omit needless words (notice that you reiterate the fact that the reading in your lit course was difficult).

—Keep looking for ways to combine sentences and to provide transitions between ideas, especially in the first paragraph.

Ellie's Next Draft

For two weeks during the summer between 10th and 11th grade, I participated in an Outward Bound expedition in Minnesota. Out in the wilderness with a group of teenagers like myself, I found myself facing several difficult situations that I could hardly have imagined before. I never thought that I'd be able to carry a sixty-pound pack for miles on a bumpy trail or paddle a canoe eighteen miles in one day. These were large accomplishments for me, who is basically a non-athlete. Until then, most of the physical challenges in my life have been optional. If I thought I couldn't run one mile, that was the end of the idea; I never even tried. But in Minnesota, I had no choice.

One day I found myself at the bottom of a very high hill with an 80-degree incline and was told to climb to the top. My first reaction was, "There is no way I can do it," but since I could not stay alone in the wilderness, I was obligated to try. My effort to climb the rock was the most ambitious I have ever made in my life. I struggled for two hours, falling many times, getting bruised, sometimes almost giving up. At times, I stopped and felt like it might be better just to let myself roll down the hill and get it over with. But I kept on maneuvering myself upward. Others encouraged me to keep going, and the guide gave me ideas about how to proceed up huge boulders and through narrow passageways between the rocks. Somehow, I found the strength to go on. In the end, I stood on the top feeling like I had truly conquered the world. My climb had been long and exhausting, but I had done it, and maybe for the first time in my life I realized that if something is possible it can be achieved.

Although I had been in Minnesota only a short time, those two weeks were the most important of my life. I was in a coed group of nine people, some of whom I didn't exactly like. But I learned that everyone can get along if they have to and as long as they all try. Thinking about the experience, I probably couldn't have made that climb without their help, and they couldn't have made it to the top without mine.

When I entered my junior year, I found that my motivation to succeed was changed. What I learned in Minnesota I applied to similar circumstances at work and school. The Minnesota wilderness had changed my approach to life. During my freshman and sophomore years, I often faced difficult academic situations. And like the unrun mile, I barely made an effort. I had no idea what I was missing. When the going got too rough, my motto was to give up. I had neither the tolerance nor the patience to learn or to try new things.

In 11th grade, however, I took an honors English class entitled Modern European Literature, which involved a huge amount of work. Although the literature was often difficult, I made the effort to read it until I fully understood it. In previous years, I would have dropped any class in which I was told I was going to read long, hard books and write several analytical papers. I also challenged myself in math, one of my weaker areas. Because advanced math courses are not required for graduation, my strong dislike for the subject tempted me to avoid them. But the new me decided to meet the challenge. Remembering the steep Minnesota hill, I knew it would not be impossible if I tried, and so I did and soon found out that once I made the effort to learn the concepts, logical mathematical thinking became easier for me.

The Outward Bound experience also proved valuable in my employment. Working as a waitress and a cashier, I interact with very demanding managers, unpleasant co-workers, and impolite customers. My patience was not unlimited. Again, I think of my Outward Bound group and how we all learned to get along and help each other. That's how I manage to deal with the pressure of the work. Regardless of the others' personalities, I stuck with the job and saved a few thousand dollars to help pay my college expenses.

I feel that in the past year and a half I have shown that I can apply this new self-confidence and motivation to my schoolwork and to everyday situations. Now I am ready to take on the responsibilities and challenges of college life and academics. I thank Outward Bound for that.

Notes to Ellie

—Much improved.
—You have made a strong connection between your experience in Minnesota and your recent efforts in school. The contrast between you in 10th and 11th grade and you at the present time vividly shows what Outward Bound meant to you.
—The details of the climb have added life and color to the story.

—If you can do so very, very briefly, try to relate an anecdote about a problem with a customer, a co-worker, or with your boss on the job. If you add words, though, be sure to cut words elsewhere in your essay. At the moment, the essay borders on being too long.

—Some of the essay is still a bit awkward. Read your essay aloud and listen for odd-sounding words and expressions. For example, check the verb tenses in the next to last paragraph.

In this version, Ellie seems to have overcome most of the earlier weaknesses in her essay. Of the five comments in the latest note to Ellie, only two tell her what to do next. Evidently, Ellie has taken previous suggestions to heart, and her next draft is likely to be her last.

Chuck D's Early Draft

In his essay, Chuck compares riding a bike to living in a competitive world. The idea has merit, but in this early draft Chuck may have been carried away by the uniqueness of his metaphor. Without realizing it, he has presented himself as a rather unappealing and ruthless character. He needs to view his essay with a new set of eyes before going on to write the next draft:

> The large brown garage doors of a small split-level home slowly creak open. Out emerges a ten-speed bicycle accompanied by its rider. He turns and shuts the large doors. As he mounts his bicycle, a shaft of morning sun peeks over the treetops and glistens in his face. He squints and slowly glides out of his driveway. The race has begun.
>
> He moves slowly along the street where he lives. As he approaches his first hill, he casually shifts down to first gear. Slowly but steadily he ascends the hill. As the horizon breaks, he spies a small bicycle about forty yards away. Like a cat stalking his prey, he increases his speed, legs pumping like pistons. His prey is unaware of his approach. Suddenly, his prey glances back and sees him only a few feet away, but it's too late. Our predator swiftly passes his prey.
>
> Who is this killer on a bicycle? He is me. We are one and the same. Bicycling to school is more than just a means of

transportation. It is yet another test of ability. It is a need. It is a psychological contest. Who can get there faster?

Why is this so? I feel that we in the American middle class are brought up to be competitive. When I see another cyclist who I know is going to the same place I am, I feel that I must try to beat him. While I may accomplish nothing by others' standards, in my own mind I have overcome an obstacle. In my mind, to overcome an obstacle is an achievement. I also feel if one achieves the goals which he sets for himself, he will, in his own mind be successful. While beating another bicycle to school is a small achievement, it can give you the feeling, psychologically, of a big achievement, possibly helping to pave the way to bigger and better achievements.

What are the rules which we all must follow? What might happen if we break them? The rules are: Be cool. Never let someone know that you know you are going to pass. Surprise is important. If the person doing the passing were making a lot of noise about it, one of two things could happen: He could forewarn the other person and put him on guard, making it harder for him to pass, or he would cause the person being passed to feel resentful because the person doing the passing would be too showy. Always pass someone without their knowing it. If you are passed, try to regain your ground quickly. If you can't within a reasonable period of time, don't bother. If one did not follow these rules, it would most likely have an adverse effect. If you were to let someone know you know he is passing you, then he would only get that much more joy out of seeing you helpless, or at least unable to compete with him.

As you may or may not have realized, this essay is not about riding to school. This essay is about a world filled with competition. Bicycling is just an example that illustrates just how competitive our world is, or at least how competitive my world is. In high school it has been competitive, and I'm certain it will be the same in college, if not more.

Notes to Chuck

—Good, dramatic opening. If possible, build even more tension—the kind you might feel before an important bike race.
—The race itself doesn't really begin until the rider spies his competition. Yet, you say it starts when the rider hits the street. Which is more accurate?

—Several paragraphs start with questions. The pattern gets repetitious.

—The paragraph about rules is long, confusing, and repetitive. Do you need all those rules to make your point?

—You seem driven by a personal code of ruthlessness, creating the impression that you are selfish, suspicious and sneaky. Do you want a college to think that about you? Would you want to have a friend with those qualities?

—Don't explain the point of your essay, as you do in the last paragraph. Let the essay speak for itself. Make the point forcefully enough for the reader to get it without being told.

—The basic metaphor of life as a bike race is clear, but you haven't fully explained where else in life you have experienced such intense competition.

Chuck's Next Draft

The large brown garage door slowly creaks open. Out into the morning sunshine a rider on a ten-speed emerges. He checks his helmet and the leg of his trousers. All in place. He glides silently down the drive and onto the street, pedaling slowly.

At the first hill he casually shifts down, then slowly but steadily ascends the hill. As the horizon breaks, he spies another cyclist just swinging around the corner onto the boulevard. He increases speed, legs pumping like pistons.

The race is on. He's like a cat, stalking his prey. Slowly the gap between them narrows. His prey is unaware of his approach. Suddenly, his prey glances back and sees him. But it's too late. He's by in a flash, his vanquished victim left in the dust.

Who is this speedster? Who is this cheetah of the road, outracing everyone who crosses his path? It is me. I am the unconquerable one. It's in my blood to race, to overcome, to win, even when it's just the daily ride to school.

Bicycling to school is not just a means of transportation. It is a sport, a contest to see who is fastest. It's a symptom of growing up in the great middle class of America. We have been bred on competition. From Little League to class rank, from college boards to basketball, winning always counts as the only thing that matters. Who is fastest, smartest, tallest, quickest, most popular, strongest, best looking, sexiest, most likely to succeed? Win, win, win says the wind. So, whenever I see another cyclist, I feel that I must try to beat him. It may seem like I have accomplished nothing, but to me it is another achievement, another obstacle overcome in the race of life.

I feel that if you achieve the goals you set for yourself, even the smallest ones, you will be successful in your own mind. While beating another bicyclist to school may accomplish nothing, it satisfies my longing to excel, to feel psychologically that I am better, faster and more ready to face the world.

I don't feel this competitive urge when cycling with a friend. Friends are for getting to know, not for defeating in a race. In friendship there is trust. Neither you nor your friend should feel the other's need to compete. If they feel the need, then friendship terminates, falling as a victim of mutual distrust.

So, the rules of life are like the rules of the bicycle race. Never let someone know you are coming up behind him. A warning will put him on his guard and make the passing more difficult. If you are passed, try to regain ground quickly, but if you can't within a reasonable period, don't try unless you know you can do it. It's better not to let the other person see you in distress, for he'll only get more joy out of seeing you helpless, or at least unable to compete with him. Then he may toy with you, tease you by slowing down and zooming ahead when you think you will pass him.

Long ago, Charles Darwin called it survival of the fittest. That's the way it was and always will be as long as we live in a competitive society.

Notes to Chuck

—At the start, short sentences and phrases create tension. You've hooked your reader firmly. Good!

—You've made yourself much more likeable in this version of the essay.

—You show that your competitive urges come from society, not from some dark impulse deep inside you.

—The paragraph about friendship adds another dimension to your personality.

—In this draft, you make your point clearly—and without specifically telling the reader what it is. Well done!

—This essay is almost ready to mail. Read it over carefully for unneeded words and for repetitive phrases and ideas. (For example, in the second sentence, "out" and "emerges" are redundant.)

After some minor editing Chuck's essay will be complete, and Chuck, being a hard-core competitor, will no doubt send it off confident that it will win him a place in the college of his choice.

APPENDIX C.
COMPLETED ESSAYS

When college admissions deans curl up to read a bunch of essays, they look for answers to two key questions about each applicant:

1. What does this essay tell us about the person who wrote it?
2. What does it tell us about how well this person can write?

The second question more or less answers itself when an essay presents a clear and accurate picture of the writer. You won't find many muddled *and* well-written portraits. Therefore, the impression you create rests largely on how vividly you are able to project yourself onto the page.

In this appendix you'll find three college essays. Each, for better or worse, reveals the writer's personality. Before you look at the brief analysis following each essay, decide for yourself whether the essay succeeds. Put yourself in the place of a college admissions officer. What does each essay tell you about its author?

Paul G

Paul, a high school senior, put on a pair of figure skates when he was eleven and has rarely taken them off since then. He is an ice dancer. He practices hours every day, enters (and sometimes wins) competitions, and dreams of skating in the Olympics. Ice dancing consumes a major portion of his time. To convince colleges that he is more than a one-dimensional person, however, he wrote an essay titled "Achieving a Balance."

> Achieving a balance on an almost paper-thin blade of steel can be a stressful experience. The first time I fell it hurt. I think of where I was then and where I am now and see my life in between as a balancing act, much like skating is, literally. The lesson I learned from falling that first time I remember: "If you stay balanced, you won't fall."

Over the next six years I learned how to stand; strong and confident. Now, spending hours a day training, I rarely, if ever, think about falling. In the beginning it was just another new sport. Now, ice dancing is a passion. However, sometimes a passion can become a misguided devotion to only one part of life. As competition and training became more difficult, keeping life in perspective grew more challenging. Increased skating demands forced me to get better organized. My mother and I spend hours driving to rinks, so I used that time to read a lot—from Cormac McCarthy to the newest Brian Jacques (a holdover from my childhood). Through it all I remained sane by staying in conventional school (competitors typically opt for tutoring or home schooling). I made time to spend with friends, continued to play tennis and baseball (despite some skating coaches' objections to playing other sports), and I rejected the notion that skaters had to live a life secluded in a rink.

My coach and friend Mikchail Zverev taught me what ice dancing really means: to skate with a partner as one and to feel each other's every move. I learned from him how to deal with inherently subjective judging by focusing on how well I skated, and then thinking about improving my skating even more. Mikchail's life in Russia had been harsh physically and politically. Because he had experienced what it was like to lose what you love, he grasped my need for staying centered—both on ice and in life. When the training got tough, he understood and helped me get through it.

There is a fullness in life that I have enjoyed because of my skating and what it has given me. But life is not all about oneself, and last year I was given a chance to start teaching a group of underprivileged girls through a program called Figure Skating in Harlem. The cold wind off the Hudson River could not diminish my enjoyment in giving back to skating. The smiles on the girls' faces, and on mine, when they achieved something new made me relish each Saturday.

Having the talent to skate has led to tough choices, but I think that trading skating for an easier, less stressful, life would have been copping out. I chose skating but rejected the baggage that too often came with it; a narrow view of life with too little exposure to the real world. The thin steel blade that had the potential to trip up my life instead led me to balance skating with learning, with other sports, with friends and family—all of which have enriched my life.

—Paul G the person has considerable self-confidence and a sense of who he is . . . has a competitive streak in him . . . realizes the diversity that life has to offer . . . knows he has a special talent but has rejected the life of a celebrity . . . takes pride in helping others.
—Paul G the writer knows how to catch the reader with an appealing opening . . . has an original mind and the imagination of a poet . . . understands how to show his many-sided personality without writing a list . . . knows how to sustain a metaphor . . . realizes that an essay's conclusion should remind the reader of the introduction . . . shows facility in writing clear English.

Peter S

At the start of his essay, Peter addresses the admissions committee directly. Writing the essay, he feels, is like fighting a battle with an unseen enemy.

It is hard for me to believe that the crucial time has arrived when I will leave the protective world of high school and enter another world as a major contestant and participant. Applying to college is my first step as a contestant in a unique kind of battle, one that is fought without blood—only sweat and tears. You, the admissions committee, become the judges. In your heads the decisive victories are won and lost. We, the winners and losers, battle one another only in words. Our minds and souls come to you in a record of scores, letters of recommendation, and, perhaps most of all, through this essay. Here you find out about the "me" not revealed in transcripts or through others' words. Each word I write represents another piece to the puzzle of my mind. How I sympathize with you, for some of the pieces may seem confusing or not even part of the puzzle.

Initially, I tried writing an essay that explained how I have been working to improve myself as a person. I grew frustrated with the difficulty of portraying the person I would like you to know, or finding an adequate way to show you my elation over the changes and growth I have experienced, especially since last summer. Now I can picture you sitting there thinking, "Well, here is another kid trying to get into our college by telling us how he has improved as a person." To tell you the truth, that picture makes me somewhat defensive. I know what this war is about: It's essay-eat-essay.

Do you remember when you feared that each word you put down would determine your future? If I had submitted my self-improvement essay, would you have been as deeply moved as I was? Would you have dropped your jaw and danced with excitement as I did when certain events happened to me? Let me try!

I have always wanted to be a more sociable person who, on meeting new people, did not retreat into a shell. Picture me *before:* One day I was stopped at a traffic light when another car pulled alongside. Inside were three of the most gorgeous examples of "pulchritude" I have ever seen. One girl about my age turned toward me. Horror! She was looking straight at me, checking *me* out just as I had done to her! I began to get nervous. Was there egg on my face? Was it April Fools'? Then the most embarrassing thing happened. She waved at me, and what's more amazing, even had the audacity to smile. My pulse went crazy. Was this really happening to me? WOW! I sure would like to meet her. But NO! I shriveled up in my seat. The light changed, and off we went into our own worlds, never to see each other again. So why didn't I wave back? Here was the opportunity I had been waiting for, and what happened? I blew it!

This experience turned out to be a valuable lesson. I began to think, "Is this the person I want to become?"

Many months passed as I sorted out many feelings about myself. During a family vacation in the White Mountains I began to realize that I had to change things that had been part of my personality for so long. I began to experiment with a "new me" during my hikes in the mountains. Each new person I met, I greeted with a hearty "Hello" and a bubbling smile. Not even totally exhausted hikers looked unfavorably at this cheerful, outgoing lad. Then it hit me! This lad was who I really wanted to be.

The new beginning: Back at the hotel I began to worry. I did not want to lose the person whom I wanted to become. I would have to work hard to assume his identity at all times. Trying out my new personality was not always successful, and sometimes the security of my old shell seemed very inviting. But then, *Success!*

I had always wanted a job in the dining room of this hotel. On the morning of our departure, I talked with the maitre d' about the mountains, about the hotel, about the dining room, about myself. No matter. Now, I knew what I was doing. I was communicating more easily, without my previous reserve. I was enjoying myself. More importantly, I *knew* there was no egg on my face! At the end of our conversation, I asked the maitre d' if he would give me a job, and you'd never guess what he said. He said, and I quote, "I would love to have someone with your personality working in my dining room!" Well, I hit the thirty-foot ceiling!

After reading this essay, did you? Probably not, for it was difficult to convey my feelings and my thinking. But I hit it. Even if my self-improvement essay did not captivate you, I know that I have, in fact, grown.

I cannot deny the past, nor do I want to. Now I feel ready to do battle. My ammunition will come from within, and any victories, as well as any losses, will be my own. I have waged a battle with myself, and I am winning. I am liking who I am. No matter what the outcome of this contest, I will keep on growing and evolving into the person I want to be. I want to hit those thirty-foot ceilings again and again!

—*Peter S the person seems a bit unsure of himself at the start . . . grows increasingly self-confident as the essay goes on, as well as in life . . . thinks that he's misunderstood—that people don't see the sensitive, complex person residing inside him . . . has a sense of humor . . . has the capacity to change . . . has the resolve to overcome personal hang-ups . . . wants to succeed . . . is sincere . . . has the courage to reveal his anxiety . . . is blessed with charm and a gentle disposition.*

—*Peter S the writer takes risks with words and ideas . . . knows how to project his personality onto the page . . . can use an appropriate story to make a point and develop an idea . . . focuses on an important personal issue . . . demonstrates overall writing competence . . . uses sentence variety and vivid images . . . gets bogged down in wordiness occasionally . . . knows how to write a strong and memorable conclusion.*

Betsy S

Betsy portrays herself with several brief glimpses into her memory. Although the images are separated by time and space, when taken as a whole, they become a finely crafted, unified self-portrait.

Certain experiences that I've had in my life have helped to shape me, along with all my schooling and all that I've learned from other people, into the person I am today. Some of them, although they may have occurred long ago, are still so vivid to me that I feel that I could shut my eyes and be there in those places again. . . .

I grasp the lifeline with my bronzed little ten-year-old hands and stretch my toes down to touch the cold Maine water. Today is beautiful, the water is calm and glistening. The boat leaves a trail of white bubbles behind it as it glides along. We were up at sunrise, Daddy and I were. At least we were up to meet the lobster boats as they went by and we got the first pick of the morning's catch. I had taken a before-breakfast swim and now my swimsuit hangs from the boom, drying in the wind. I turn my head back, lean under the jib, and wave to my dad who sits holding the tiller with his bare foot. My mother sits near him, reading a book, my sister is sunbathing, and my little brother is play-ing with the hermit crabs that we've adopted as pets. My father beckons me back to the cockpit and lets me take the tiller. I stand with my bronzed, proud little ten-year-old face gazing up, over the cabin, off at the horizon . . .

The tears flow down my face, faster still as I glance at my sister and brother, their faces tearstained too. It seems so ironic to me that, at eleven years old, I am standing in the most beautiful restaurant in New York, in the most elegant dress I've ever owned, and I am experiencing the most pain I've ever felt. My father glances over his shoulder at us, even as the ceremony is taking place, and I see the pain in his eyes too. I think of my mother, alone at home, in the huge, new house that he just bought for us. What will she have done when he drops us off tonight? Last weekend she tore up their wedding picture. She's broken some dishes and called him every rotten name right in front of me. Inside I've called him them too. I'm only eleven years old and I'm so confused. I love my parents both so much and I'm not ready to have these feelings. I hardly even know this woman he's marrying . . .

I wake up, having slept for the shortest four hours of my life and I force my eyes open and I crawl to the shower as I shampoo my hair. My brain begins to function again and I think to myself, "Any sane person is going to the beach today, sleeping until noon, and wouldn't think of touching a schoolbook." After my shower, I go back to my room and Lindsey, my roommate from Toronto, and I get dressed in a hurry. Grabbing our books we run down the stairs and out the door of our dorm to walk to breakfast. On the way to the Commons, we begin to meet all our friends. It has become a daily ritual, these past weeks at Andover. First we see the kids from Stevens East and Taylor Hall hiking up the hill. Soon we see Jennifer and Dana coming across the quad from Day Hall. We walk into the Commons, grab some Cap'n Crunch and a glass of O.J. and walk over to join the others at a table. I sit back and listen to everyone. They're complaining about their homework, the lack of sleep, the food, the strict curfews, and chattering about our next trip to Boston, letters from home, the newest couple, and I smile at Lindsey and our looks say to each other, "When have we ever been this happy before?" . . .

I stand at the top and lift my face up toward the sun. I take off my sunglasses and lean forward onto my poles. I feel every muscle in my body, every muscle in my legs, my shoulders, my arms . . . A pacific, white sea lies in front of me. There's not another person around me. I'm skiing better than I ever have before. I'm concentrating on every move as if in slow motion. I feel so close to Heaven and so down to Earth. I feel a remarkable energy, maybe from the sun, maybe from the center of the Earth, flowing through me, making me glow. Everything inside me, in my head, seems to come together and I am whole. I lift my face toward the sun and I can't help but smile as I think to myself, "This is me. This is what I am."

There are so many other examples that I could choose to show who I am, many of them are not vivid images of memorable moments, but everyday parts of my life. I love to walk down the hall at school, talking and joking with almost everyone I pass, teachers and students alike. I love the feeling I get when I tutor someone and I help them to understand a concept that they couldn't quite get on their own. Most of all, I love to sit at the kitchen table and talk with my mother and her fiancé, or to go out with my close friends and laugh and hug and know that we can always lean on each other. I work hard and I play hard. I spend a great deal of time studying my books, but also a lot of time forming relationships with other people. I want all the beauty that life can give . . . all the knowledge, all the love. So I fill up my cup and I drink it in.

—*Betsy S the person loves life and appreciates its possibilities . . . feels and thinks deeply . . . searches below the surface for the essential meaning of everyday occurrences.*
—*Betsy S the writer has a rare gift for saying what she thinks and feels . . . has composed an essay that deserves to be read again and again.*

APPENDIX D.
STUDENT CONTRIBUTORS*

Elissa Greenberg Adair, Princeton

Chandra Bendix, MIT

Joel Berkowitz, University of Pennsylvania

Ian Biederman, Northwestern

Deborah Brause, Tufts

Brian Cunnie, University of Pennsylvania

Peter Davis, Johns Hopkins

Roger Denny, Columbia

Teresa DiMagno, SUNY Binghamton

Charles DiMicco, SUNY Albany

Sabrina Eaton, University of Pennsylvania

Ellie Ehrenhaft, Ithaca

Susan Epstein, Yale

Lisa Estreich, Harvard

Susan Faulkner, Brown

Ellen Gamerman, Swarthmore

Paul Goldner, Harvard

Alicia Grant, SUNY Binghamton

Maria Guarino, Fordham

Alexander Harrington, Columbia

Lawrence Harris, Franklin and Marshall

Eric Hecker, University of Pennsylvania

Elizabeth Humphrey, Fordham

Alison Lipow, University of North Carolina

Thomas Mackenzie, University of Colorado

Steven Maddox, Harvard

Jon Martin, Cornell

Sally McCauley, Smith

Pamela Meadow, University of Pennsylvania

David Miles, University of California, Berkeley

Michael Miller, New York University

Tracy Parker, Carleton

James Reilly, Duke

Annette Rogers, Boston U.

Elizabeth Schmidt, University of Michigan

Peter Scotch, Connecticut College

Andrew Smith, Washington U.

Gina Smith, Syracuse

Linda Wiereck, Oberlin

*Several contributors chose to withhold their names or to be listed under a pseudonym.

INDEX

Notes

Notes

Notes

Notes

Notes

Notes

Notes